Praise for *The Pact: Messages from the Other Side*

"Every once in awhile you read a book that takes you beyond the edge of the known and into the timeless realm of the soul. *The Pact* is one of those special books. It takes the reader on a spiritual journey through life after life, weaving a tale of relationships that is like a Navajo rug. Seen from the bottom, there are multiple threads. Seen from above, a pattern of stunning beauty emerges, a story of love that is stronger than death. Dr. Sinor and her departed husband's personal life pact unfolds as a spiritual memoir that uplifts and inspires, uniting past, present, and future."

~ Joan Borysenko, Ph.D., New York Times best-selling author

"*The Pact* is a profoundly intimate and poignant account of a deeply loving couple whose love and connection remain true and flowing across time, space, life, and death. I have never seen a book about channeled information written in quite this way and it strikes me as very effective and moving. *The Pact* provides a clear example of the phenomenon of channeling, and the spiritual education and satisfaction that can come from recognizing ourselves as eternal beings with many lifetimes of growth and experience."

~ JP Van Hulle, Michael Channel, author
Michael: The Basic Teachings

"*The Pact* grabbed me deeply and fully within my physical, emotional, mental, and spiritual bodies with validity and confirmation to my own intuits and perceptions. *The Pact* assisted me in my own expanded conscious awareness of my Oneness with All That Is, God Source. The book will validate many questionable feelings for others, as it did for me. Thank you, Barbara and David, for your courage to write this book and present it to humanity. The way you brought many of your lives together and how you showed the connectedness is phenomenal."

~ Reverend Ruby M. Morrow, Astara

"Sinor weaves together a tapestry of exotic narratives from her lifetimes (past lives) into her present life journey, blending themes of living, loving, dying, and believing. Depending on how the reader approaches *The Pact* will determine the lessons gleaned from it and their degree of impact. This, I believe, is the beauty of the book. Although my belief systems vary greatly from Sinor's, I resonated with her enduring love story that transcends eternity. With her timeless connection to her earthly departed husband, Sinor's writing gifts readers with a path to healing and most importantly to hope."

~ Holli Kenley, M.A., MFT, author
Mountain Air: Relapsing and Finding the Way Back
...One Breath at a Time

"*The Pact* is a beautifully written illumination of the thin veil between souls and incarnations. We truly do walk within, beside, and toward one another every step of the way. Highly recommended!"

~ Jeff Brown, author
Soulshaping: A Journey of Self-Creation

"Dr. Sinor's *The Pact* weaves together a story of a lifetime of love, and also explores the past lives of this devoted couple. Anyone with questions about what it is like when we cross over to the Other Side will find the question and answer portion at the end of the book both fascinating and thought provoking!"

~ Kay Fahlstrom, author
Reborn a Medium: A True Story of Dying,
Returning, and Serving Spirit—and You

"*The Pact* brings the reader an adventure of many lifetimes with the clarity of a personal energetic connection between two souls. The stories are filled with tears of truth and a laughter of knowing beyond words which seem to call spirit inward for recognition. Thank you, Dr. Sinor, for sharing the intimate details of the pact which was made between you and your husband."

~ Reverend Peggy Tennent, Astara

"*The Pact* is a fascinating book... an engrossing page-turner. It enlightens the reader to the reality of the journey of the soul on various planes of existence. The book increases the understanding of who we are spiritually and what is in store for us after we have moved from our current lifetime. As a longtime psychotherapist and regression therapist, I appreciate the depiction of several of the author's lifetimes. Sinor beautifully interweaves the theme of abiding love through her accounts of her current life with her husband; their previous lifetimes; and, the communication between them from the other side."
~ Barbara Lamb, M.S., MFT, CHT, Regression Therapist, author
Crop Circles Revealed

"*The Pact* discusses the author's past lives and how her loved ones' souls interact from lifetime to lifetime. It is a very personal and in-depth exposition of reincarnation that coincides with lives from Eastern, Western, modern, and ancient histories. The book also describes God within us and the relationship with our soul. *The Pact* is a must read for those interested in the subject matter of karma and reincarnation."
~ John Smethers, Ph.D., author
Addict to Academic

"*The Pact* is a beautifully written account of communication with one who has passed. In a thought provoking way, Sinor relates a journey of lifetimes with her husband, and in so doing, assists us in asking the question, 'Can we also communicate with our loved ones?' Sinor helps us to lighten the veil between ourselves and the other side and to assist us in our search for answers about our own path on this journey of lifetimes. A wonderful book!"
~ Rev. Patricia Haller, Unity Minister

"My soul was touched by the energy of the words from *The Pact*. I have been a transpersonal psychotherapist for over thirty years and I know Truth. The forever lasting love that is shared in this book informs us about the world beyond the physical realm. I highly recommend it."
~ Susan B. Cohen, MFT

"Most of us only get a glimpse of our karmic trail in the life we are living; yet in *The Pact*, Dr. Sinor offers some of her soul lineage via channeling from the other side. By dancing back and forth, past and present, the reader indulges in a time machine effect that is entrancingly entertaining. I found the overall thread of past lives to not only be credible by way of interconnectedness to other souls, but also by virtue of the fact the author consistently pursues healing people both physically and psychologically. The different lifetimes will fascinate the reader from a myriad of experiences and historical viewpoints offering a window into many interesting cultures that have long since passed. Only a seasoned veteran of authoring multiple books could weave such an enlightening manuscript. I highly recommend *The Pact: Messages from the Other Side*."

~ Celeste Palmer, author,
The Follies of Free Love

"*The Pact* truly is a healing book and I am glad Barbara has shared her story with us. While I don't believe anyone can fully confirm whether or not reincarnation occurs, to me it makes more sense that people reincarnate, not because of negative karma or as some form of punishment but by their own choice as a learning experience that propels the evolution of their souls. Whether you've always been interested in reincarnation, have never before considered it, have been hurt by religion in your past, are a religious skeptic, or are seeking to understand your life's meaning and purpose better, you will find much to consider in *The Pact*, and if you read with an open mind, I am confident you will come away enlightened, perhaps healed of pain, and better equipped to live your life to its fullest and fulfill your own incredible mission on this earth."

~ Tyler R. Tichelaar, Ph.D., award-winning author
Spirit of the North: a paranormal romance

The Pact

Messages from the Other Side

Barbara Sinor, PhD

Marvelous Spirit Press

Distributed by New Leaf Distributing, Ingram Book Group
(USA/CAN), Bertram's Books (UK/EU), and other fine wholesalers.

2nd Printing - April 2014

Library of Congress Cataloging-in-Publication Data
Sinor, David Lee (Spirit)

Sinor, David Lee (Spirit)
    The pact : messages from the other side / Barbara Sinor, Ph.D. -- 1
[edition].
        pages cm
    Includes bibliographical references.
    ISBN 978-1-61599-213-3 (ebook) -- ISBN 978-1-61599-214-0
(pbk. : alk. paper) -- ISBN 978-1-61599-215-7 (hardcover : alk. paper)
    1. Spirit writings. 2. Reincarnation. 3. Sinor, David Lee (Spirit) 4.
Sinor, Barbara, 1945- I. Sinor, Barbara, 1945- II. Title.
    BF1301.S623 2014
    133.901'35--dc23
                                    2013047484

Published by Marvelous Spirit Press, an imprint of

Loving Healing Press, Inc.   info@LHpress.com
5145 Pontiac Trail   Tollfree 888-761-6268
Ann Arbor, MI 48105   Fax: 734-663-6861
www.LHPress.com

Contents

Introduction v

Channeling ix

One 1

Two... 9

Three 17

Four 29

Five 37

Six... 45

Seven 55

Eight 65

Nine 73

Ten... 83

Eleven.. 95

Twelve.. 107

Thirteen.. 119

Channeling: David's Story of Heaven 127

Channeling of Lifetimes.. 157

Author's Note 169

Lifetime Identification Chart 173

References 175

Illustrations 177

About the Author 179

We are not offered guarantees.
What we are offered is knowledge of life and ourselves;
And if we are awake,
glimpses of the wisdom held in the story
our life is telling the world.

from *The Invitation*
by Oriah Mountain Dreamer

Barbara Hutchins Sinor

Introduction

Beyond the reality of our daily lives, busy with getting an education, raising a family, and securing employment to sustain our desires, there is a spiritual life silently unfolding. Our spiritual views are as diverse as the people on this planet. Different types of spiritual and religious beliefs possess words and rituals used to sustain each system that brings people together for the sole pleasure of worshipping a Divine Source. Even if one does not have a spiritual belief system, *that* is a spiritual belief in itself.

Belief comes from our mind, a human concept that is guided by our physicality, or brain. The renowned theoretical quantum physicist Amit Goswami stated so clearly, "Consciousness is the ground of being—not the brain. The brain is made of consciousness, but consciousness is not made from the brain." Whatever your belief in the nature of being, there can be an appreciation of open-mindedness to the concept of a soul's progression after death. Spiritual teacher Ram Dass explores this topic openly when he writes:

> People ask me, "Do you believe that there is continuity after death?" And I say, "I don't believe it. It just is." That offends my scientific friends no end. But belief is something you hold on to with your intellect. My faith in the continuity of life has gone way beyond the intellect. Belief is a problem because it is rooted in the mind, and in the process of death, the mind crumbles. Faith, consciousness, and awareness all exist beyond the thinking mind.

During my life, I have been fortunate to have the opportunity to explore many of the religious views found on Earth, and I find they ultimately covet sisterhood and brotherhood through Love. Whether or not a religious system proclaims a belief in reincarnation, we must ask ourselves the same questions. The Theosophical teachings, founded in 1875, provide some of these spiritual ponderings: How can we believe that souls are created at a certain point in time, and yet, they live forever? How can a soul survive the body, but not pre-exist it? How can one soul live for over seventy years within a body, then drift into insignificance at the death of the host body? Perhaps questions such as these will never be thoroughly answered to our satisfaction, but you may find some answers within this book. My chosen belief system encompasses a broad view of East and West thinking, which has sustained my compassionate and positive attitude toward all life. My late husband and I had made a pact that whoever passed away first would connect with the other to confirm, or not, our belief in an afterlife and my belief in the existence of reincarnation.

The writing of *The Pact* has been a collaboration between me and the channeled words of my departed husband. For those readers who are not familiar with the concept of channeling, it can be accomplished through techniques such as mediumship, automatic writing and drawing, intuitive sensory perception, and various other means. I channeled my husband's words during meditations that can be found in the chapter "Channeling David's Story of Heaven." In Chapters Thirteen and Fourteen, I offer this personal process in more detail. At the back of the book is a glossary of the lifetimes shared in this book called the "Lifetime Identification Chart." This chart can be used to help guide you through many of my soul's adventures.

Let me attempt to answer the eminent question you must be thinking: How did I receive the channeled words so clearly from my departed husband? As I sat at my computer each session, I allowed myself to leave my body insomuch as to join with the silence within my mind. In this state of consciousness, I closed my eyes and listened only to the birds singing outside my office window. I also realized a not-so-silent inner-ego, which I found I had to tame to make sure I did not change any of David's channeled words. Here is where I met my beloved—between the worlds. I released all form of doubt, all fear of failing to hear David's words stream through my mind. When I had allowed myself to be in this frame of silence… David's words tumbled into my senses. His words came like a flood, targeting their own destination of my waiting fingertips posed gently, but firmly, against the letters of my keyboard.

As you read through *The Pact*, keep your own spiritual mind open.

Search your inner self for answers to the many questions your mind will no doubt put before you. As each story touches your heart, allow your own lifetime review to surface. Tap into your inner consciousness as you unfold and search your dreams, visions, and meditations, which may visit you more vividly while reading this book. *The Pact* is a gift from me to share with those who decide to take a journey to explore the reality of reincarnation.

Barbara Sinor, Ph.D.
March 1, 2014

Channeling

We will always be with you... always near you, just ask and we are here beside you. Your book will be a great comfort to many. You can use your lifetimes to share with others and show how our free choices direct our growth. It will be read by many who will use the information for their own guidance. Weave a tale of love, Barbara... for your lifetimes have been evolving in grace and love.

Tell me more about our lifetime together in Atlantis.

Our lives during Atlantis were of two women cave-dwellers who had reached the highest regard as healers. We lived during the era of the *Trine Crystal* named for the huge three-sided pyramid crystal discovered in one of the largest caverns. We were sisters, and as one unit, we healed those from the caves who needed us. During our lifetime, the Trine Crystal began generating an abundance of power; the lands began to shake, causing enormous water tidals, which surrounded the island. The entire continent was destroyed, sinking into the oceans. Our lives were filled with love for each other and the sharing of our healing powers. We did not live long; our lives were cut short in the destruction of the island of Atlantis.

What were our names?

Your name was Athena and ours was Meratta.

One

When the deep meaning of things is not understood
the mind's essential peace is disturbed to no avail.
                                        Chien-chih Seng-ts'an
                                        Zen Patriarch, 606 AD

"Athena? Meratta? Where are you girls?" the old woman
called into the evening air. Shaking her head she thought,
Those girls! They are always running off together!
"Athena? Meratta? It's time to come home!" she shouted out again.
When will they ever learn it is not safe to be outside after the sun falls?
she thought to herself as she turned to walk back down the stone steps
into the cave-dwelling.

Athena and Meratta were very busy, unaware of anything except
their search. They had not noticed the sun dipping below the tip of the
great pyramid, for they were gathering more herbs to use as teas to
help heal the families living in the caves.

"Here's a new one!" Meratta exclaimed as she held up a tiny clump
of greenery. "I think it is the one Amma told us would heal the hot
sweats of the elderly women. I will take it with us and ask her
tomorrow."

"Oh, that is definitely a new one, Meratta!" replied Athena, inspect-
ing the leafy green shoot.

"Oh no!" shouted Meratta as she pointed to the sun rays falling in
an array of colors. "We have been outside too long, Athena; we must
gather our things and return home quickly."

Athena and Meratta watched one last time the setting of the sun
and its glowing rays of yellow, pink, and red. They packed their
baskets tight with the day's findings. They were not far from their

cave-dwelling and had faintly heard the calls from their mother, but as usual, they ignored them to pursue their passion. They loved their mother, but they knew she did not understand their strong desire to learn the ways of Amma, and how to heal those who were not well in the caves.

Once safely up the hill and in front of the stones leading to the opening of their home, Athena whispered as she pointed to the valley below, "It is so beautiful. Do you think we will ever be able to visit?"

"I hope so," Meratta replied as she swept a finger across her forehead to remove the blonde strand of untrained hair obstructing her view. "Even if we never get to see the lighted valley, I will be happy here learning more from our dear Amma."

"Yes, I agree with your words," Athena said softly as she gazed lovingly into Meratta's blue eyes. Slowly descending the stairway, the pair of blossoming young women vanished into the darkness.

Athena and Meratta were sisters who lived with their mother in one of the caves surrounding the impressive community of Atlantis with its shining lights, water canals, and huge gardens filled with fruit trees and all variety of foods. When they were younger, their mother would tell them stories about the times long ago when the love beings came from the sky to offer instructions to their people about the ways of bringing-into-view with their minds. Many learned how to *bring-into-view* the needed instruments to make the large domed dwellings and how to light the night sky. Each person who wished to learn the new lessons would be given these abilities. The people learned to develop the wonders of illuminating the night sky and the magical ways to use stone and marble to form their pyramids in which to learn other mysterious ways. As their mother told these stories over and over, the sisters would sit quietly at her feet, absorbing all the visions of the strange land.

Athena and Meratta also met Amma when they were young. Amma was a wise elder with white-gray hair, dark penetrating eyes, and a soft deep voice. Her presence silently commanded respect as she seemed to float across the ground with a soft glow emanating around her body. Amma came one day with a few others to the sisters' cave, crossing the perimeter of the Atlantis community from a larger cave that went deep inside the earth. Their mother was ailing and Amma instinctively knew she was needed. Her trip was an arduous one for the old woman, but her mission was of healing all cave-dwellers surrounding Atlantis, so a bit of walking and hiking did not deter her ambition.

"Where are you distressed, my dear?" Amma asked their mother as she searched for a small bowl shaped from knottelwood tucked at the bottom of her basket.

"My head is spinning, and when I try to stand, I fall back down," replied the girls' mother.

"My, my... not to worry, my dear. Amma knows what will heal you." She spoke in deep comforting tones, soft, like the tender grasses outside the caves.

Amma reached a second time into the large mysterious basket packed tightly to the top. When her hand emerged, in it was the most beautiful flower Athena and Meratta had ever seen. Amma instructed Meratta to render a gourd of water heated by the center fire. Then she poured the water into the wooden bowl, gently placing the flower at the bottom. She stirred it with her fingers while talking softly to their mother. The girls could not hear all that was spoken, but the words seemed to settle the lines in their mother's face.

The next day, Amma said it was time for her journey home. She told the girls to tend to their mother with the warm water and flowers she had left them. After placing the flowers in a smaller basket, she handed it to Meratta and said, "You and Athena will one day be healers as I. I will come when the moon is full each cycle to teach you the ways," and with that said, Amma left with her companions.

❧

"Athena, do you think Amma will come tomorrow at the full moon?" Meratta asked as they walked the pathway trod so many times by the cave-dwellers. She held her basket close to her, not wanting to lose the unknown treasure she had found that day.

"I know she will, Meratta; she always comes to teach us the healing ways on the full moon," Athena said as she led the way on the winding stones.

"I can't wait to show her our new finding! She will be so pleased with us, I just know it!" Meratta shrieked as she touched the moist stone wall near her head to steady her way.

Arriving at the crossway, they turned to the left toward their home to find their mother busy cooking over the center fire. "Guess what we found today, Mother?" Meratta exclaimed.

"Well, whatever it is, I hope it was worth your staying out to the sun's passing!" their mother admonished.

"Oh it is, Mother... it is!" beamed Meratta with excitement as she reached into her basket to bring forth the prize of the day's search.

"Look, it is so pretty even without a flower!" Meratta said, holding the leaf toward the fire's light for her mother to see.

"We were well within our time to arrive at our cave before the lights would shine in the valley, Mother. Do not worry; we will be careful always," assured Athena.

"Well, let me see your leaf," said their mother as she came closer. "Ah, yes, it is a lovely one indeed! I am sure Amma will be happy with your finding."

"Will Amma be here for sure tomorrow, Mother?" inquired Meratta with a tenuous voice.

"Oh, yes, I am sure she will, my dear Meratta. She has much more to teach you and Athena... she will be here," she said affectionately.

The three ate supper and soon settled down for the night's sleep with excitement in their hearts to meet with Amma once again the following day.

Athena, with her long black hair loose down her back, turned on her side, facing the dark stones she knew so well. Many times when she went to bed and the center fire was still bright, she would count the cracks in the stones and trace them with her fingers to other small breaks that formed the pieces that took the appearance of faces, animals, and flowers. Once when she could not sleep, Athena recounted the many designs she could find, savoring the fact that only she knew of all the stories hidden in the stones.

Meratta slept close to her mother with her hand resting gently upon her breast. Just knowing her mother was near was a comfort for Meratta. She was younger than Athena and fair-skinned like the water lily petals found near the canals of Atlantis. Of course, being the younger sister had its benefits and rewards. Meratta was always allowed her say, no matter what the topic or how wrong she might be in understanding or discussing it. Her light blue eyes would sparkle at the slightest excitement, and she possessed a gentle smile, which she shared with everyone. Meratta was shorter than Athena, who was taller than most women, but a sturdy girl with a laugh that echoed through the caves.

The sisters were very close, mostly because they both had a passion to learn the healing ways. Most days, they could be found together just outside the cave-dwelling up to their knees in green shrubs and thickets of berries. Once they witnessed their mother's healing by Amma, the two sisters were determined to be healers like their mentor.

Amma did arrive the next day with new herbs and flowers to share. But before she could even take a breath to relax from her hike, Meratta shouted, "Amma, look what I found yesterday!" Meratta took the small bunch of greenery from her cherished basket and placed it on the tall stone in front of them.

"Oh, my... my... this is a wonderful finding, Meratta! It is a rare finding with many healing abilities," Amma told her softly to calm Meratta's over-excited state.

As Amma took the greenery into her hand, she touched each leaf as if to impart a magical healing quality to its deep texture. "I will show you how to use this finding tomorrow. Now, let me rest for a little while and talk with your mother," Amma told Meratta.

Meratta and Athena waited patiently as the two women talked of the stories heard from other cave-dwellers throughout the hills. It sounded to the sisters like there was something happening in the community of Atlantis that was most exciting. When the conversation stopped and Amma came to sit by them, Athena asked, "Can you tell us of the excitement in the community in the valley, Amma?"

Amma began her story. "Many suns and moons have passed since the beginning of the community called Atlantis. Your mother has shared much with you about the great division of people formed between those who now live in the caves and those who live in the community. Before the people of the community had their huge stone dwellings and bright lights, there came large beings from the sky with the highest of knowledge. They had the ability to use their minds to produce everything they desired. They saw a struggling settlement down upon our land where people used twigs and sticks to form huts in which to live. The beings witnessed caring people who lived a physically difficult life and they decided to teach these people the ways of their homeland. The people of the valley had the opportunity of learning from the beings how to use their minds to develop their needs and change their lives. Many people did learn from the visitors how to manipulate with their minds, while others did not. Soon the visiting beings left and the settlers in the valley formed groups. The groups were divided—those who could use their minds to create and those who could not."

Amma took a long breath and then continued with her story, "You girls only get glimpses of the community of Atlantis when you are out searching for your healing herbs and berries. Those people who did not learn to envision with their minds became cave-dwellers such as you

Illustration of Plato's Atlantis

and I. Our people have lived many lives in the caves, learning and teaching each other the ways of healing, growing food, and using the many tools the caves have given us."

"What tools?" asked Meratta with twinkling eyes.

"The tools I am going to share with you today. I am sure you must have seen many forms of these tools already," Amma said. She dug with her gnarled hand into her basket to reveal a cloth folded neatly around items only imagined by Athena and Meratta.

"Oh, do share now, Amma! I am too excited to wait any longer," Meratta said as she once again pulled her unruly strand of hair from her face.

"Yes, my dear, look here...." Amma removed the cloth to expose the cool smooth crystals lying inside. "When you pass the caverns of your cave, did you notice any of these stones?" asked Amma.

"Oh, yes, Amma. I know of several places in the caverns where this type of stone can be found," Athena responded with an eager tone. "They are not as shiny or smooth as these, but are the same type of stone I am sure."

"These stones are called crystals. They can be used to heal others by placing them over, around, or upon one's body. I will teach you both how to use all these crystals, and you will then know many of the ways of healing that I have learned."

"Oh, thank you, Amma!" shouted Meratta as she jumped up to share the news with her mother who was sitting by the center fire.

"Athena? Look my way, dear one. I am giving you these crystals to keep and learn to use wisely. They have many powers that I will teach you and you will share with Meratta. Let us begin," and with that, Amma rewrapped the smooth stones, except for one, into the cloth and handed it to Athena.

❦

As Athena became a young woman, she never forgot the special day when her dear Amma had entrusted the healing crystals to her care. Through the years, she and Meratta learned their powers and soon journeyed together each day to help their fellow cave-dwellers return to wellbeing and strength. They both learned how the crystals could be placed evenly around and across the body in different patterns to direct their healing energy. They intuitively learned to use the correct crystals at just the right time in each healing process. But most importantly, they learned from Amma how to take their crystals to the largest cavern in the far hills to renew them with powerful energy.

After many moons, while Amma was showing the young women how to mash the goji berry with the root of anise, she told them the story of the great Trine Crystal.

"Gather near, girls, so my voice does not carry beyond your ears. Soon I will take you on a journey to the cavern near my home in the far hills. There you will witness the mystery of the great Trine Crystal and revel as I once did when seeing it for the first time. The great crystal has enormous powers, enough to fill all your healing tools for the rest of your lives, as well as, to provide the secret energy for the community of Atlantis. It has been told that long ago the sky beings deposited the great crystal into the cavern where it has remained to bring light to the valley. Our people found it by accident while hunting for healing tools. They discovered that by placing each healing crystal tool near the Trine Crystal, it would fill with greater power than before." Amma adjusted her robe, took a deep breath and continued her tale. "So as my mother shared this with me, and her mother shared with her... I am sharing this with you."

"When can we leave?" asked Athena bravely.

"Within the next six moons, my dear one," replied Amma; then turning to Meratta, she whispered, "We will have a great journey together, just the three of us!"

Meratta clapped her hands and gave the old woman a hug. "I just knew there was something special about the great cavern we have heard about from others. I will go tell Mother of our plan." Meratta then jumped up to go in search of her mother.

"Amma, why is there not a great crystal for our people?" asked Athena with a concerned stare.

"Dear child, our people chose to live in the caves. They knew they would not live fairly beside those in the community and, therefore, chose to make a life away from the stone dwellings. We have had our trials, but our knowledge of the land, sky, water, plants, and animals is all we need to live in peace. One day, I will tell you the story of the strife and discord in the community below and how it hangs heavy on the people who live there. But for now, let us talk of healing! Where did Meratta go? She needs to be near to learn the mashing of the berries!" Amma said more loudly than usual, and then she rose from her sitting position to glance sideways in search of Meratta.

Two

To deny the reality of things
is to miss their reality;
to assert the emptiness of things
is to miss their reality.

Chien-chih Seng-ts'an
Zen Patriarch, 606 AD

I awoke with a jerk and kept my eyes closed so I would not forget the dream so fresh in my consciousness. As I lay in bed remembering the visions of a lifetime from so long ago, I gently opened my eyes while reaching for the pen and tablet I had purposefully laid out the night before. Eagerly, I began to write. I wrote for hours early that morning and again late into the night. I knew from past experience that if I did not go-with-the-flow of a writer's vision, it would be tucked in the recesses of my mind to be lost forever. I wrote down all I could remember of the convincing dream I had experienced early that morning.

Again, I questioned whether I was crazy, or at the very least delusional. I gazed in the mirror, disappointed to see the aging woman who lived there. Combing my thinning blonde-white hair, I stopped to study the wrinkles around my eyes. At least the years had not robbed me of my smile; I took a quick second to smile back approvingly at the mirror's unfamiliar reflection. *Was I chasing dreams like they were the magical potion for eternal life?* I thought to myself. *Was it a lark to believe David could actually send me visions of our lifetimes together?* I turned to place the pen down on the night table to organize a new tablet showing a blank page ready to accept another story from my dream world.

That evening before retiring for bed, I took out Tablet #3 to peruse its contents. I began to read out loud the first words handwritten with my favorite black inked pen: "Athena? Meratta? Where are you girls?" the old woman called. After reading through most of the tablet, I edged toward believing the dreams were sent by my departed husband, as proof of our lifetimes together.

David and I met when I was just fifteen years old. At the time, I was not sure I should even be talking to him over the neighbor's hedge. He came regularly to work in our neighbor's yard. I could tell he was much too old for me, maybe even out of high school. But, each time I heard his noisy lawnmower's motor, my heart stopped. Then it would begin beating so fast that I thought it would pop out of my chest! I would quickly go outside to watch my reflection in the large front window while practicing my cheerleading moves. I did my jumps and yelled out all the high school cheers, well knowing I was being watched. I did my best to impress the glances I was receiving from over the hedge. This ritual went on for several weeks through the early summer when I was quite bored. I actually enjoyed going to school, and when summers came with their three-month school break, there seemed to be a sense of limbo to my life—but not in the summer of 1961.

After several weeks of cheerleading displays, David waved over the hedge he was trimming and said, "Hi! What's your name?"

I stopped my cheerleading yells and came closer, saying, "Hi, what did you say?" I could only see his head and shoulders above the hedge.

"I said, 'What– is– your– name?'" he asked again.

"Oh, well, I guess it's okay to tell you, even though I really don't know who you are… it's Barbara," I said very coolly while also trying to smile.

"Well, I see you all the time outside doing your cheers and wondered if you wanted to talk," David said with some hesitancy.

"Oh, well, I don't know. I don't know who you are…" I retorted.

"My name is David. There, now you know who I am. Are you a cheerleader at the high school?" he asked fairly.

"Yep, this is my first year at it. I was just chosen and I start next year when school starts. I am not as good as some of the other girls, but I am trying to teach myself. My older sister was a cheerleader too, so she has taught me some of the moves," I rambled and then stopped, realizing I had revealed quite a bit of information to a boy I hardly knew.

"Well, I think you are very good, Barbara!" he said with a big smile that drifted into a little crooked smirk on one side.

"Thanks, David. Well, nice talking with you," I said turning to go back to work on my jumping techniques.

I always enjoy remembering how I met David for the first time. In fact, lately I find myself thinking of all the good times we have had together. I would lie in bed and envision all the exciting trips and adventures we shared for so many years. *Has it really been that long since my beloved David shut his eyes to this life?* I now thought. My eyes began to swell with tears; I could never seem to control them when I was thinking about him. I was getting sleepy and my expectations to float into another dream urged me toward my bed.

I set down the tablet I had been reading. Then snuggling down under the covers, I closed my eyes and once again whispered into the darkness, "Good night, honey. Send me more lifetimes of our souls' lives together."

And the dream continued...

✍

"Come along, Meratta, you are too slow and lagging behind us," Athena insisted as she motioned her arm forward.

"I am coming; I am coming... it's just so hard to pass all these beautiful flowers and not pick each one!" Meratta exclaimed.

"Amma? How much farther is your home?" Meratta asked.

"Not much longer now, dear ones. Keep the pace, as we must not be seen by those from the valley. And keep your voices lowered," Amma directed.

"I will. I will," Meratta repeated in a hushed tone.

The small group had been walking all morning and into the day; everyone was excited, yet very tired. The sisters had never journeyed so far from their hills before and were in awe of the views and newness of the land. They witnessed a variety of plants they had never seen and were delighted when Amma would stop to explain their names and healing qualities. Each sister chose many different berries, plants, and flowers to tuck into their beloved baskets, excited to learn of their healing abilities.

There was a faint path to follow through the shrubs, as if it were trod only occasionally. They were told not to veer off this path or they might get lost in the thick underbrush. The sisters were overjoyed that it was their time to venture beyond the caves in the hills where they lived. Their lives had been blessed with such a loving mother to watch over them and teach them the ways of living comfortably. Both of the sisters had learned how to make the center fire, dig for roots and bulbs, catch the shelled crab near the water channels, and carve out the food bowls with pointed stones. Athena and Meratta inherited their mother's gentle nature and grew to be loved by many in their caves. They felt truly blessed, indeed.

To Athena, however, nothing compared to the journey with her dear Amma to visit her home and the great Trine Crystal. Athena had always felt she was special. She would envision experiences before they even occurred and knew exactly where to go to find the right herbs and berries to heal an ailing body. She knew she was to learn many other healing methods in her life. She wanted to learn all she could before Amma became too old and frail to teach her ways. Athena also knew that one day she would be the highest healer of all the caves, taking Amma's place when the time came.

"We are almost home, *my* home, dear ones. Just over that ridge and up the hill," said Amma, pointing in the direction they were to hike.

"Will we arrive before the sun passes below the great pyramid?" asked Meratta with a slight note of apprehension.

"Yes, dear child, or should I say, young lady! You girls have grown so quickly before my eyes. I am happy we made this important journey together," Amma said as she reached out for the sisters to come to her breasts for a hug.

"We are the fortunate ones, dear Amma. We are very pleased to be your students and will listen to all you share with us," Athena promised.

"Yes. That is why you were chosen out of all the girls your age. You and Meratta have the needed passion to learn the ways of healing... and will surely learn a great deal tomorrow!" Amma said excitedly.

As the group continued hiking up the hill, Athena asked, "So tomorrow, when the moon is full, we will visit the crystal pyramid in your cave?"

"Yes my dear... tomorrow," Amma answered.

Amma needed to sit for a few minutes at the top of the hill to breathe deeply and relax her tired body. The three sat on large stones along the cliffs of the cave's entrance to gaze out over the valley and watch the sun fall slightly beneath the tip of the great stone pyramid of Atlantis.

"All right, young ladies, let us walk the inner path to my home where we can eat and rest until the morning," Amma instructed, and gathered her basket.

❧

The following day, Athena and Meratta awakened to a sound they had never heard. A soft muted tune sang in the air above them. The chime was hung high over their heads and the gusts through the cave made it dance with its metallic findings. This delighted Meratta so much that she jumped up from her sleep coverings and ran over to watch the shining objects that reflected the flames from the center fire. She hummed with the notes as they echoed upon the stone walls of the cave.

"Amma, Amma, what is this pleasing treasure that dances with a song?" Meratta blurted out just as Amma was waking up.

"Well, good morning to you too, Meratta. Let me open my eyes a bit before all the questions come to me across the floor." Amma took a deep breath, then another. She closed her eyelids and sat still for several moments to center herself. Directing her attention back to Meratta, she said, "Your body would do well to calm itself in the mornings before the day becomes rushed. Come; sit with me a few moments and see what I tell you." Amma patted the covered sleep area next to her for Meratta to sit.

"I am so sorry if I awakened you, Amma; I was just so excited to hear the sounds," Meratta whispered to her mentor.

"Yes, yes, I know dear. No harm is done. The chime is made of bits of findings I have discovered along the pathways leading down to the community. Now, you and Athena listen as I tell you how to calm your inner life." Amma placed herself between the sisters and sat with legs crossed. The sisters knowingly did the same.

"When it is time for life to re-enter a body after sleeping, it is wise to be still and ask life what it must do for the day. To do this, we first close our eyes. Now, take a few deep breaths and let the air out through your mouth very gently and slowly like this," Amma said as she demonstrated what she was instructing. "Now you try it."

Athena knew exactly what to do, for she had watched Amma do this often. She closed her eyes and began to do the breathing exercise. Meratta was a fast learner and soon was sitting quietly doing the breathing Amma had taught them.

"Dear ones... dear ones? Do you hear my words? You have been quiet for long enough, and we must start the day," Amma gently urged.

Meratta and Athena opened their eyes and to their amazement saw the morning's food laid out before them. "How did you prepare our food so quickly, Amma? Did you use your magical powers?" Meratta asked.

"My dear one, it is you and Athena who have touched your magical powers. You have taken a long rest to calm your inner life as you sat with your eyes closed breathing in and out like the pumps from the community's canals. Once you calmed your inner life, your outer life became quiet. I want you to do this each morning for the rest of your lives; do you understand?" asked Amma, facing both the sisters.

"I felt like I was floating inside, Amma. It was a most peaceful place to go, and I will surely go there each morning upon my waking," Athena replied.

"Yes, I too felt a peacefulness within me. I cannot believe I sat still so long!" Meratta exclaimed with eagerness to try it again, but Amma insisted they must eat so they could start their journey for the day.

"Your caverns are so much larger than ours! They seem to go forever Amma!" shouted Meratta as she followed behind the two women.

"Look around, Meratta; you may find new healing crystals here. I have found all the ones I use and those I have given to you and Athena in this very cavern. When you find them, put them in your pouches that I gave each of you at the start of our journey this morning," Amma instructed.

"Yes, I will, Amma. Look over there! There is a stream of glistening water! How did it get inside the cavern?" Meratta asked, looking puzzled.

"There are waterfalls and streams all along this cavern; it is where the people in my caves get their water to drink. Up ahead, through there, is the great Trine Crystal," Amma said as she pointed with one hand and wiped her brow with the other. "This is a sacred place; please keep your voices to a whisper. Also, we do not want to cause noise to arouse the people from the community. There, over that way, can you both see it?" Amma inquired with excitement.

"Ohhh, Amma... I had no idea it was so large!" Athena whispered, "It is the most beautiful thing I have ever seen! Can we get closer, Amma?"

"Oh yes, please, let's get closer!" Meratta whispered in agreement.

"Yes, my dear ones, follow me now, very closely." Amma motioned forward with her arm.

As they followed the twisty path close to the cavern walls, Athena felt something deep inside her—a comforting feeling. She put her hand over her heart and felt the life energy inside. She felt connected and whispered ahead to Amma, "My heart feels full, Amma, like a peaceful knowing. I feel calm and excited all at the same time."

"That is exactly how I felt when I first glimpsed the huge crystal, Athena. There is certainly a connection from deep within. I know you are to become a high healer, my dear," said Amma as she also placed her hand over her breast.

"How much closer can we get, Amma?" asked Meratta eagerly.

"Close enough to place our healing crystals at its base. They will stay for one moon cycle, and when we return, the crystals will be filled once again with renewed energy," Amma said.

"So we are to return again and find them here?" Meratta reaffirmed what she had heard.

"Yes, dear one, you will make the journey with Athena at the next full moon, and I will be waiting to show you the way once again to the great Trine Crystal," Amma declared with authority.

"Why is it called a *trine* crystal, Amma?" asked Athena.

"Trine means *three*, Athena," explained Amma.

"Can I walk around it to see the number of sides?" Athena inquired, hoping Amma would answer, "Yes."

"Yes, you may go all the way around it now that we have gotten close, but first let us place our healing crystals down at its base... over this way. Follow me now, for there is not much room to place your feet. Also, do you feel the warmth?" Amma asked the sisters.

"Oh yes! Can we touch it?" Meratta asked.

"No... do not touch it! It may be too warm for our hands to be touched. Now, remove your crystals from your pouches and carefully place them over here by my own. Just over here," Amma said, "is where I placed mine at the full moon last, so I will take those with me now." Amma walked a short distance from the sisters to retrieve her healing stones and tucked them safely back into her cloth pouch.

"Now, may we walk all the way around it, Amma?" asked Athena.

"Yes, I will wait here for you. Remember, do not touch the great pyramid crystal and watch that you do not slip where the path is narrow," Amma said lovingly.

Athena and Meratta held hands as they started off on their secret mission to walk around the great crystal. They giggled, then remembered to be quiet as Amma had instructed. When they came to the narrow part of the path Amma had warned them about, Athena took head-point and Meratta followed closely.

"This crystal must be at least two caves in walking. It is the largest, most beautiful thing I have ever seen," whispered Athena.

"Oh yes, sister, Mother will not believe us when we tell her of the great Trine Crystal," said Meratta.

Soon the sisters returned to the place where Amma was sitting, waiting for them. She held out her hands above her head and said in a hushed voice, "Is it not magnificent?"

Three

*Be serene in the oneness of things
and such erroneous views will disappear by themselves.
When you try to stop activity to achieve passivity
your very effort fills you with activity.
As long as you remain in one extreme or the other
you will never know Oneness.*

Chien-chih Seng-ts'an
Zen Patriarch, 606 AD

After writing out the dream that had continued from the night before, I wondered whether I should do a search on the computer about Atlantis. I knew many people believed there had been a continent named Atlantis, but I really did not know much about its history. I had heard that some people even thought it might have existed a million years ago. *My goodness*, I thought, *David certainly must have all the knowledge in front of him to be able to send me this detailed lifetime!*

I began to read what I had written in the tablet, knowing there might be some clues to why David had sent me the information about this lifetime. David had told me which sister I had been in that lifetime, but I felt I knew intuitively as I first began to read it. When I studied the words I had just written, I felt a deep calm within me, like a warmth had entered my being. "Is that you, honey?" I asked the air in front of me, and then turned my head to look in every direction to see whether I could spy his form. Nothing appeared, and with a slight sigh, I closed my eyes to rest.

Suddenly, I opened my eyes and realized I had nodded off to sleep. I glanced at the round clock hanging over the dining room table and was astonished to find that two hours had passed! Shaking my head to one side and then the other, I mumbled, "Awww, getting old is the pits!" As I rose to fix my supper, I began to remember more of the Atlantis story from the dream and quickly walked to the bedroom night table to retrieve Tablet #5 from the drawer.

I sat down and began to write once again...

"Athena? Meratta? It is getting late!" The sisters' mother voiced her familiar call from the cliffs of the cave. Her hair was gray now, and many lines resided upon her face. Her daughters had warned her not to come to the cliffs to call for them; they had told her they were now old enough to know when to come home on their own. But their mother had always walked the stones to the entrance of the cave to call for them, and even though the walk became more difficult each day, she needed to continue the routine.

"Athena? Meratta? I am going inside to lie down. Please hear my calls and come inside for the night," she called one last time, and then turned to walk back down the steps to her familiar cave-dwelling. This time, she needed to grasp the stones along the walls to find her way; her weakened body was failing. She did not let her daughters know of the pains in her side; she did not want to worry them. *Besides*, she thought, *they have done everything possible with their healing tools and herbs to tend me.*

"The moon will be full tomorrow; will Amma come for a visit *this* time?" Meratta asked Athena as they gathered their day's findings.

"Yes, Amma comes this full moon; we travel to her on the next one, remember? Why is it that you cannot remember the easiest things?" Athena replied with a spark of sass in her voice.

"I guess I don't try hard enough like you do, Athena. But remember, we are both to become high healers; that is what Amma said," Meratta turned from Athena in a quick movement, accidentally bumping Athena's basket and spilling its contents on the ground.

"Oh, no! Look what you have done, Meratta!" shouted Athena as she bent down to pick up her treasures.

"I am so sorry, Athena. Sometimes I don't know what is the matter with me! Sometimes, I don't feel like a healer at all," Meratta said as she bent down next to Athena to help her retrieve her findings.

"Meratta, look at me. Look at me straight in the eyes. You are a beautiful young woman with many healing talents. Never feel inferior to anyone! I love you dearly, Meratta. I think I am just worried about

Mother," Athena admitted.

"I know; she has not been well lately. We have used all our crystal tools and herbs to heal her, but she doesn't seem to be getting better. I hope Amma will help her tomorrow," Meratta said with tears in her blue eyes.

"As do I, Meratta. It is getting late; we have to hurry to reach the cave before the sun falls," Athena said as she quickly stood up straight. "Let us journey home now and no more talk of who is the better healer."

When the sisters arrived in their cave, they found their mother lying down and no food was prepared for supper. Immediately, they both knew something was terribly wrong. They kneeled over their mother to see whether they could tend her. "Mamma? Are you feeling ill?" asked Athena as she bent down to her mother's face. Her mother's eyes did not open. "Oh, Mamma! Are you no longer here with us? Has your life left us?" she screamed.

"Oh no, that cannot be, Athena. She is just resting before she begins making our food," said Meratta assuredly, and then she came closer to inspect her dear mother's face.

As the sisters touched their mother's shoulder and head, they knew her life had left her body. They held each other and cried for most of the night before drifting into a fitful sleep.

Amma arrived early. She knew what she would find when she entered the sisters' cave-dwelling. She outstretched her arms wide to receive both Athena and Meratta's willing bodies. They shared their stories together until well into the day. When Amma knew it was time to wrap their mother's body tightly in a large cloth, she called for the other cave-dwellers to come mourn the life that had left them. They placed flowers and crystals all around the still body in a blessing of love.

The next day, many people came to look upon their dear mother's face one last time. Then the decorated body was carried through the caves to the opposite opening where the waters splashed the cliffs below. These waters were not to drink, but only to accept the bodies of those who had left their lives in this land. All the people sang of love and motherhood, and then Athena and Meratta recited the final "Blessing of Motherhood" that had been told by many families before them. Together, they recited the poem as they placed their hands over each breast:

Our mother's love was strong and pure,
Our mother's love was kind and sure,
Our mother's love was patient to the end,
Our mother's love will always be within.

After they had finished the poem, their mother's body was placed in the ropes and lowered down into the salty waters.

Amma returned with Athena and Meratta to their home and stayed with them for several nights. She shared with the sisters the ways of life leaving a body, just like the birth of life that comes with bringing a baby into being. She told them of a different kind of land that receives a life that has left this one. After the talks with Amma, the sisters felt a wonderful sense of calm about their mother leaving her life to go on to another.

"How shall we manage alone, Athena?" asked Meratta. "We have not needed to learn many of the ways of preparing food and sharing it with the other people of our cave. I am afraid we have been too busy learning the healing ways."

"We will manage, Meratta… "Athena began, only to be interrupted by Amma's words.

"You both will come with me to my home. It will be easier for me to teach you… so it is done," and with that, Amma began gathering items to take on the journey.

"Oh, how wonderful!" shouted Meratta. "That is a generous offering. Can we go with Amma, Athena?" she asked, turning toward her sister in a pleading manner.

"Oh yes, dear sister, I agree this is the best plan," replied Athena.

The sisters took their time gathering their treasures and the cloth to wrap them in, and then they quickly piled the rest of their items into a large basket. Amma had instructed them that they were to take only the belongings they could carry themselves; she would send others for the remainder of their items.

The three healers began their adventure upon the path that led around the community in the valley once again. The way had become more familiar to Athena since traveling it several times to visit Amma and the Trine Crystal. She knew exactly where she could find the needed herbs and berries she liked to use to help heal those who were ailing. She also knew what to expect when the path narrowed so only one body could walk at a time. Athena had become a beautiful woman with her black hair tied up tight against her head with a thin cloth and then flowing down her back. Her body was straight, tall, and muscular, unlike Meratta's, which was shorter and thin-boned. *They were like night and day*, Athena thought as she led the way up the hills to Amma's home.

Living with Amma, the sisters were able to learn quickly the healing ways that Amma taught so wisely. They went out together to many surrounding caves to tend to those who lived in them. They became the high healers they so wished to be as young girls, and Amma was proud. During their outings, the sisters ventured closer and closer to the community in the valley so they could inspect its inhabitants' unusual ways. They were curious to learn more about these people after Amma had shared her stories of how they lived and fought together. Learning about fighting among people was disturbing to Athena, and especially to Meratta, who would not hurt a flea. They had always lived in a land of peace; their people never raised a hand to one another. Once when the sisters had ventured too close to the valley, they had heard the shouting and seen the people running after each other. They had really not known what to make of it and quickly turned away to get back to the safety of Amma's home.

Even though Athena and Meratta had traveled to the great Trine Crystal many times to lay their healing tools at its base, they were always a bit awestruck when they came upon its glowing structure. *There is a presence to it, as if it were alive*, thought Athena as she placed her healing tools down and picked up the ones she had left on the full moon past. Then turning to Meratta and pointing upward, she said, "Do you find yourself wondering what it would be like to touch it?"

"Oh no, Athena! We must not touch it. Amma would be very upset with us," she retorted.

"I know, I will not touch it. I was just wondering what it would feel like. Would it be hard like a stone, or would it be soft like my healing wand that Amma made for me? Do not worry, my dear sister; I will not disobey our sweet Amma's instructions." Athena turned and started the long walk back to Amma's home, which had also become their own. Sometimes, Athena would search her mind to remember the home they had in the caves across the community with their mother, but the memory had weakened; both of the sisters so enjoyed living with Amma and learning all her ways.

Amma knew she was reaching an end-point to her life as high healer, and she did not journey with the sisters to heal the ailing people of the caves any longer. She knew they all were being tended with the very best care by the sisters whom she had taught so well. Amma fixed her braided gray hair to one side, tied it with a thin cloth, and began adding more wood chips to the center fire. When Athena and Meratta returned home, Amma motioned for them to sit beside her, for there was something important to discuss. She took one long deep breath, closed her eyes, and relaxed her aging shoulders.

"Athena, Meratta, I have something important to share with you. I have known for several moons that there will be a day soon when our land, and the community in the valley, will no longer be...." Her voice trailed off, and then she resumed, "I tell you now, for I have felt a terrible darkness inside. I do not want to alarm you, dear ones, but you should know my truth and try to feel it too."

Athena began the discussion without hesitancy, for she too, had felt something deep inside that she had not understood. Now she understood, and replied, "Yes, Amma, I too have felt it. I did not know that the shadow I have felt hidden within me was this truth, only that darkness was near."

"Well, I have not felt anything as you discuss, but I take your words as truth," stated Meratta, trying to sound unafraid.

"When is this to happen, dear Amma?" Athena asked her mentor.

"When the moon is full next, there will be a disturbance in the great Trine Crystal and our land, and our lives with be no more," Amma recounted with her eyes closed as if to find the information from deep within her.

"We must prepare," Athena asserted.

"Yes, dear ones. We must let all the cave-dwellers know of this truth and also to prepare," Amma instructed. "Go out to the caves and spread the words of our discussion."

"Meratta, get yourself ready; we will leave tomorrow morning when the sun peeks over the tip of the great pyramid in the valley." And with that said, Athena rose to gather her newly energy-filled healing crystals and other items to make the journey. "Will you go with us, dear Amma?" she asked as she turned around to help Amma off the sitting stone.

"No, my dear ones; I cannot make the journey. I will wait for your return before the full moon, so we can be together," replied Amma with a touch of sadness in her voice.

"We understand," Meratta said as she, too, guided her aging mentor to the center fire for warmth.

The following day, the two sisters of high healing went about the caves to share the discussion about the darkness coming to their land. All the people received the news well... almost as if this inner knowledge had been sent magically from mind to mind. The following full moon, the sisters once again set out to visit the great Trine Crystal as they had done religiously. Once they arrived to place their healing tools at its base, they could feel the discord—a new energy unlike any they had ever felt. Also, there was an emanating purple beam glowing from the tip of the pyramid that went directly up through the top of the cavern.

"We must hurry, Meratta; we must go be with Amma!" Athena needed to shout over the mysterious noise beginning to fill the cavern. She grabbed her crystals and placed them hurriedly into her basket.

"Is the end of the land near, Athena?" asked Meratta as she followed her sister's lead.

"I fear it is so. Let us walk faster than ever before to reach our dear Amma!" Athena shouted again.

Once safely in their home, they found Amma preparing to take the walk to the cave's entrance. "Where are you going, Amma? Is not the darkness we have felt inside now beginning?" Meratta asked as she assisted Amma by cupping a hand onto her right elbow for balance.

"Yes, dear one. I fear this is the truth that we have told the others," Amma replied as she continued her steps. "We must hurry if we are to see the sun set one last time."

Arriving at the entrance to Amma's large cave, the sisters stopped on the cliffs to gaze upon the setting sun. They so enjoyed watching the colors as they dissolved into one another to form unique shapes and textures. Then... the land beneath them started to shake and loud noises came from deep within the cave. Athena yelled to Meratta and Amma, "Come with me; we must get off the cliffs!"

"No, my dear ones. We can stay here and watch the beauty of our land one last time," Amma tenderly said to the sisters as she motioned for them once again to come to her breast.

The noise became louder as the ground shook the stones from the sides of the cliffs. Athena firmly held her footing to be able to hold on to her sister and Amma. They all placed one of their hands over their ears to help shut out the loud noises around them. They saw the green valley shaking like waves below them, moving like the outside waters where their mother's body had been lowered. Athena looked up toward the sky and saw dark smoke sailing down toward the massive valley floor. Then she witnessed white fire streaming upward from within the top of the mountain where the great Trine Crystal had been placed so long ago by the visitors.

"Come, Meratta; hold me tight, for I fear we will leave our lives this day…"

❧

I had tears in my eyes as I placed my pen and tablet down. Whispering to David, I said, "Oh honey, what a special lifetime that was… it's just so sad that it ended as it did. That makes two lifetimes our souls have shared in which our lives were cut short. I wonder, were there others?"

Looking back down at Tablet #5, I patted it on its cover and closed the pages. I knew I needed to eat supper, so I wiped my eyes with a tissue to refresh my tear-streaked face and began to heat a portion of the vegetable soup I had made the day before. As I stood in front of the stove, waiting for the soup to heat, I thought back to David's and my life together.

David and I became one of those young couples you see in romantic movies. After several times of talking over the neighbor's hedge during those sunny summer days, David mustered-up enough courage to ask me out. I wanted to go on a date with him, but I wasn't sure my parents would approve of me going out with an older boy with his own car and everything. But when I told them about David, how we met, and where his family lived, they both approved.

I was so nervous when David knocked on the door for the first time to take me to dinner. My stomach was nervous, my heart was pounding, and my mind could not stop shouting things *not* to say or do while being with him. We talked over our dinner in a fancy restaurant I had never been to, and the date ended with us sitting in his big green Oldsmobile in front of my house. We must have talked for hours because it was really late when we finally said good-night at the front door, and he gave me a kiss I would never forget.

David was in college just as I had guessed. He was working as a gardener to raise the money he needed for books, fees, and the gasoline and oil he needed for his car to drive to the college several towns away. He was very handsome at nineteen years old; his hair was almost black and cut in the popular "buzz-cut" of the '60s. It was either this type of hair cut, or the longish Beatles look, which would not have suited him at all. His eyes were also dark and he stood only three or four inches taller than me. I thought David was quite a catch with his husky

1961 - Barbara, Paula, and David

muscular body and little crooked smile. His parents' house was only a few miles from mine; he was still living with them, his two sisters, and an older brother. He called me on the phone every day, even if he could not be with me. He told me years later that he fell in love with me the first time he saw me.

I will never forget one date, late at night, when David drove us in his big Olds out to the cow pastures. We lived in a small farming town with many dairies. He parked the car off the side of the narrow road, turned off the lights, and asked whether I wanted to make-out in the back seat. Of course I did! So we both settled in the backseat and proceeded to get hot-and-heavy, about second base… fogging up the windows. All of a sudden, a big white light shone through the window! We didn't know what to expect. I was terrified it was an escaped prisoner from the nearby men's prison. Then, there was a loud metal tapping on the window and David rolled it down just a few inches. A police officer was standing on the other side of the window with his flashlight, peering into the car to look around. "Okay, kids, time to wrap it up and go home now," he ordered.

"Okay, officer," David obeyed, glancing at me to suggest I button my blouse. Thank goodness the officer left before we returned to the front seat because I was not eighteen, so David could have been put in jail!

Our love grew stronger each year, and in the fall of my senior year, David proposed and placed a diamond ring on my finger. We were married in less than six months. We were young and in love and that was all that mattered to us. David chose an apartment in a nearby town and we moved my bedroom furniture into it; and soon, we bought a living room sofa, tables, and even a new television. David worked every weekday for a contractor, while I stayed at home to cook and clean the little apartment. Sometimes, I would get up early to take him to work so I could use the car to go see my girl friends or go shopping. Once, just before I left to go pick him up from work about thirty minutes away, I put a whole chicken in the oven so it would be ready to eat when we returned. We returned late and that night we ordered pizza—the chicken was charred black.

After a few years, I desperately wanted to have a baby. My mind was set on a boy and a girl. When I was a teenager, I had picked out a name for a little girl, Cindy. I felt this little soul near me for many years, knowing she had picked me to be her mother. While I was waiting to conceive, I had to learn to drive a stick shift because David

Our 1959 Chevy El Camino

sold what I had called The Big Green Bomb. He bought a 1959 Chevy El Camino with four-on-the-floor. Poor David tried to be patient with me grinding the gears while I was learning to drive his new treasure. Sometimes, when I was trying to change gears, he would crouch down in the seat so no one would see that he was also in the truck!

In the late 1960s, David received the official government letter—he was drafted. My heart sank, knowing he would probably be sent to serve in the Vietnam War we had heard so much about. We put all our furniture in storage and I moved back into my parents' house. David rode the provided Army bus into Los Angeles to get his instructions. Late that same day, he showed up at the front door! He had not passed the physical exam because of a curvature in his spine. He was disappointed; I was happy. We needed to live with my parents for three or four months until we saved enough money to rent the next little house that we moved into a few towns away.

Soon, we were able to buy our first house. We were both very eager to start our family and could not wait for me to become pregnant. The house had three bedrooms and two bathrooms. It was bigger than any of the homes either of our parents had ever owned. We were ready for baby number one.

When I finally got pregnant, David did not believe it! He literally did not believe I was pregnant until he placed his hand on my stomach a few months later to feel the movement of the tiny life within me. Our first baby surprised me; it was a boy. We named him Richard Wyatt Sinor, using my father's middle name for Richard's middle name also. Richard's name soon turned into Richie, and that is what we called him his entire life. Richie was a smart and happy baby and little boy. Less than two years later, I gave birth to the baby girl I knew I was supposed to have in this lifetime. My life was full, but having two children so close together was a handful. They were both in cloth diapers (disposables weren't around yet) for almost one year until I could get Richie potty-trained. Soon, our life with two kids was perfect. We would go on trips camping, fishing, hiking, and to ride the dirt bikes David bought for himself, Cindy, and Richie.

Oh no! My soup was boiling over! I had once again lost myself in the old memories that came so easily. I added a bit of rice milk to temper it and ate supper once again, alone.

Four

The Way is perfect like vast space
where nothing is lacking and nothing is in excess.
Indeed, it is due to our choosing to accept or reject
that we do not see the true nature of things.
Live neither in the entanglements of outer things,
nor in inner feelings of emptiness.

Chien-chih Seng-ts'an
Zen Patriarch, 606 AD

"Richie's drunken behavior is coming between us; can't you see that honey? " I spoke softly.

"But he's our son. What would you have us do—throw him out to live on the street?" David asked.

"No, I don't want that... but when is he ever going to grow up? We can't keep giving him money and buying his clothes and vehicles and medicine and...." I paused, not liking the resentment welling up inside me.

"I know. Maybe just this one last time, and he will finally get sober enough to keep a job and get out on his own," David said.

"All right, tell him he can stay here a few more months to get his strength back, just so he can go find work and a place of his own," I said, giving in.

David and I had learned to put up with our son's demands for many years, but now we both were recognizing just how much of a toll it was taking on our own relationship. Rich had begun drinking early, in his high school years. His buddies introduced him to alcohol and his double lineage of alcoholism from his grandfathers kicked in fast until he was hooked. As the years passed, Rich became a full-blown alcoholic, which came with its own set of demands. He would occasionally confide with one or both of us about his trying to keep sober, then relapse, which put him in a sinking depression that would continue the cycle of drinking all over again.

David and I were trying hard to keep our marriage intact as we labored to encourage our son to remain sober. We had even stood by him through several rehabilitation stints, DUIs, court hearings, hospital stays, and many times, we fronted him the money needed to get established to live on his own. Finally, Rich stayed sober long enough to be hired by a great construction company. He moved out of our home and into a small cottage to begin his new life. For most of that year, Rich remained sober by going to meetings. At forty years old, he finally slew his alcoholic demon and was happy with his life.

David and I reveled in the way Rich had become so knowledgeable in the work he was doing. He also helped us with remodels and much of the maintenance to our home. This was a great help because David and I were beginning to age a bit and could not do everything we used to when we were younger. Just as life seemed to settle down for all three of us, Rich injured his back.

Rich's little cottage had a narrow crawl space that could be accessed to replace pipes, cables, and so forth. One day, when he was trying to maneuver under the house to hook-up a washing machine, he twisted his body and felt a sharp excruciating pain shoot up from his lower back. He managed to get out from under the house and lie down. He put an ice pack on it, and then reached for his cell phone. "Mom? I just broke my back! It really hurts; I think I really did something major to it!" Rich tearfully reported through the little phone. "Can you come over?"

"Oh, no! I am so sorry, honey," I assured him. "I'll be right over." I grabbed my purse and drove the twenty minutes to his house and found him stretched out on the floor in severe pain.

"I think you need a trip to the doctor, Rich," I said. "I'll call to make an appointment to get you in as soon as I can. In the meantime, use the ice and try to do a little stretching to see if that helps."

The doctor's appointment, and the subsequent MRI, revealed several herniated discs in his spine. Rich needed to be scheduled for an appointment at the University of California Spinal Center in San Francisco. His doctor felt he needed surgery. He said the center would call Rich to schedule an initial exam appointment within a few weeks. It was difficult for Rich to manage on his own during this time, so

David and I went to his home each day to check on him. Rich was given pain medication, but he did not want to take it, fearing the onset of a physical addiction because he was a recovering alcoholic. He decided to take over-the-counter pain medications instead, which did not seem to alleviate the pain very much.

Four weeks went by, but still no call from the UCSF Spine Center. I became infuriated and called Rich's doctor, leaving a not-very-nice message that we had not received the promised call. He returned my call, stating that he would put in a second order, and added, "The scheduling might take longer because Richard is a MediCal patient."

Rich had not worked long enough to receive medical benefits from his new employer, so all his medical expenses fell upon the state's medical support system called MediCal. We all became frustrated with the long wait, especially since Rich was in such terrible pain. David and I did everything we could to help him with shopping for food, cleaning his house, and driving him to medical appointments. I even tried to call the spinal center directly to inquire about the delay, but I could not get past the recorded messages on the opposite end of the phone. The day arrived when Rich could not tolerate the pain any longer—he started drinking, hoping to dull the throbbing nerves in his back.

The center never did contact Rich, or his doctor. Rich could not work; he could barely walk because of the pain—and the amount of alcohol he was now consuming. David and I watched as our son became an active alcoholic once again. He lost his home, truck, and most of his possessions. He moved into a small trailer with a casual friend, and sadly, this is where David found his unresponsive body.

I snapped out of my memory-recall with a jolt as the teapot whistled its piercing screech. I jumped up from my reclining chair without putting the leg rest down and almost fell over onto the floor. "Darn chair!" I shouted, turning backward while shaking a finger at the inert piece of furniture. I fumbled to get my cup of hot tea, and then settled back down in the chair, keeping the leg rest down. Out loud, I whispered, "Honey, are you there? We sure had a difficult time with our son, didn't we? Why did it need to be so hard?"

My voice trailed off…. I thought I heard David's voice coming from his recliner in the corner of the room. I looked in that direction only to see an empty chair filled with memories. Again, I questioned, "David, have we had other lifetimes with Richie? Lives without so much drama and pain?" Then I thought, I sure hope so because this one was terribly traumatic for all of us!

As I sat sipping my herbal tea with lemon, I began to wonder whether David could also send me lifetimes that we all had shared. I had requested, before he died, that whoever passed away first would send the remaining one information about lifetimes we had experienced together. David and I both agreed this could be done through any means possible from the other side, such as dreams, psychics, visions, mediums, automatic writing, or any other form of communication. David was not sure he believed in reincarnation, but he agreed to our pact.

Again I thought, *If David can send me the detailed lifetimes through my dreams as he has been doing, why can't he direct me to lifetimes with Rich too, maybe even Cindy?* I started to get excited with the thought of learning about more of my lifetimes, and the possibility of finding out whether we had experienced lifetimes with our children's souls before this current one.

I walked to my bedroom to search through the tablets describing my potent dreams and the lifetimes David had channeled to me from the other side. I picked up Tablet #1 to reread.

"Anna Jo? Can you come play?" shouted little James while wiping his nose with the left arm of his pale green shirt.

"Let me ask Papa, James," Anna Jo shouted back from inside the small box-shaped house.

"'Kay... I'll be... waiting," James' voice trailed off in a thought of how he wanted to take Anna Jo down to the creek bed to look for frogs. It was the perfect time of year to find really big ones. He began making circles in the dirt with his right shoe and noticed a small hole starting to form on the bottom.

James and Anna Jo had known each other most of their lives, and they lived only a few houses from each other. Their homes were two of the several makeshift cabins offered by the Virginia colony's former Governor Berkeley to ensure tenant farming families would not live unsheltered. Both James and Anna Jo's parents qualified because Anna Jo's father was a valued tobacco plantation owner's stable hand, and James' mother was a widow. Anna Jo's family was of German descent, with her grandparents coming directly from Germany to settle in the Pennsylvania Dutch colony. Her father, John Brackston, was a large robust man who loved working with horses. Anna Jo's mother had died giving birth to her, which was not uncommon in the early 1700s.

John's original family name was Braxton, but after his wife died, he traveled south to the western area of Virginia, and wanting to start a new life with a new name, he changed it.

Anna Jo ran outside, dressed as usual in coveralls, ready to explore the day with her best friend, James. She was about to turn seven years old and was excited to learn whether James remembered the day was coming soon.

"Do you want to go down by the creek today to look for frogs? I bet we could find a big one!" James smiled his big grin, showing several spaces where missing teeth had fallen out to make room for new ones.

"Oh yes! That would be fun," Anna Jo replied as she, too, smiled to display vacancies where new, larger teeth would soon reside.

The two walked hand-in-hand around the little cubed houses to the cool creek and sat side-by-side for a moment before getting down to the business of frog hunting. James' dark head of thick hair and Anna Jo's white-blonde curls sticking out of two pig-tails, made the pair look like opposite pieces from a chessboard waiting to be moved. Their little hands still entwined, they sat for a long time in silence, watching the pebbles at the bottom of the creek try to stay their ground as the rippling undercurrent urged them to travel down the bed to a new location.

"I bet I can find the biggest frog!" Anna Jo yelled to James as she made her way down to the cool water. She had worn her high boots her father had given her for her birthday last year. They were a little tight, but she knew they would be the only boots she would have for several years. Stepping into a puddle of soft mud, she exclaimed, "Watch out! The ground is really soft over here!"

"Oh no, Anna Jo, don't ruin your boots; let's take 'em off," James suggested, as he sat down to remove his own worn shoes. James knew his mother would be very upset if he came home with muddy shoes.

James' mother, June Ann Livingston, had been widowed before James was born. June had been married to one of the famous English Livingstons who came to the new world of the Americas seeking exploration and excitement. When they met, he was preparing to travel over the rugged range of mountains in the West. He had obtained fur trappers to guide his party, wagons and horses, and found several other men looking for adventure to accompany him. The couple had only been married a few months before he left, never to return. Several months later, his party was found; they had all frozen to death. James' father never even knew his wife was going to bear him a child.

Anna Jo was already knee-deep in water, searching under rocks and the bush that draped over the edge of the old creek bed. The bottoms of her coveralls, which had been tucked nicely in the top of her boots, were now soaked.

"Oh, Anna Jo!" shouted James as he made it into the water near her. "You didn't take off your boots and now they are terribly wet. Won't your pa get mad when you get home?"

"Oh, I'll dry them out when we catch our frog," Anna Jo replied with assurance.

As the pair slowly continued their search, flowing downstream with the waters that swirled around their feet, they saw colorful fish with bellies striped with colors of blue and gold. But they were not looking to catch fish that day, just the biggest frog they could find. After several hours, James asked, "Should we give up? I don't think we're gunna find any frogs today, Anna Jo."

"Well, it has been quite a while now and my feet are getting terribly cold," Anna Jo stated as she lifted up one of her legs to reveal her soaked boot. "Maybe we better get out; I need to dry my boots before Papa sees them!"

As the two climbed out from the creek, James took Anna Jo's hand and they began the hike back up the incline toward home. Once they arrived where they had started, Anna Jo sat down in the grass and removed her wet boots. The weather was warm that summer and her boots would dry quickly. While they were waiting, James threw small round stones into the creek to show Anna Jo how strong he was. Even though James was a few months older, Anna Jo was much taller, by a full head. It was necessary for James to show her that he could do anything she could do. "Let's see who can throw rocks farther," James said, shouting above the noise of the creek.

"'Kay..."Anna Jo shouted back as she got up and ran to his side.

"Here, you go first," James said as he gave Anna Jo a large rock.

Anna Jo took the rock and threw it hard into the creek, then turned to James and said, "Your turn."

James found the perfect rock, just a bit smaller than the one he gave Anna Jo, and threw it far over the creek bed to land several yards on the opposite side. "There, I win!" James said with a grin.

"Yep, you are a strong boy, James," she said and patted him on the shoulder. "We better get home now. Papa will be looking for me."

❧

My eyes were getting tired again. I took off my reading glasses, placed the tablet on the table, and decided to watch a little television. As I sat in bed, propped-up with pillows behind my back, I turned on the screen mounted at the opposite end of the room. Flipping the channels, I found a movie, a romance. I definitely have a romantic soul. I watched the movie with my eyes, but my mind traveled back to my own courtship with David.

David became a regular at the Hutchins' dinner table. Through our years of dating, he was at my parents' house as much as his. It was fun for me to watch David as he ate something new which his mother had never cooked. Once when my mother served artichokes, David looked at his plate and laughed, "Do you really eat this... and how?"

"Well," I instructed with a grin on my face, "just take a leaf off like this and dip it into the melted butter. Then use your teeth to scrape the meat off." After showing him the technique, I continued, "Be sure not to eat the pointed ends with the little prickly needles!"

David gave it a try, and then wiping the butter from his chin, said, "Oh, that's good! So, I just eat all the leaves? That doesn't seem like very much."

"Well, when you get to the center, there is a heart and you can eat that too. Some people use mayonnaise for dipping, but we like butter. Wait until you taste the heart; you'll love it!" I said while eating my own leaves and then discarding them in the large bowl placed for everyone to use in the center of the table.

David's family did not go out to eat in restaurants, but my family made it a regular outing almost every weekend. So, of course, David was usually invited. Another type of food he had never eaten was one of my family's favorites—Chinese. We needed to drive all the way to the next town to find a Chinese restaurant. It was filled with Buddha statues, Chinese paintings, and gongs. Our family of five, plus David, would sit in one of the big round booths and share all the dishes that turned on a rotating block of wood in the center. It was fun to explain to David what all the new dishes were and to see which ones he enjoyed.

David was also a romantic and would give me flowers and cards on holidays, and especially on my birthdays. During those dating years, his libido became more difficult to manage, so we did everything we could to delay the inevitable. In that era, it was not acceptable to have sex before marriage like it is today. My mother did not offer much insight into what I should or should not be doing, so it was up to us to stop our make-out sessions before they went too far. This was very difficult for David, but also for me who yearned to give myself to the one I loved. One night when everyone in the house slept, we approached the too far point. I whispered, "We have to stop doing this! It just isn't right and we can get into so much trouble. Let's think of a way we will always remember to stop when we start to go too far."

"Awww... well, I guess," David slowly agreed.

"I know. Here's a penny on the coffee table," I said as I picked up the little piece of copper. "I am going to put it up on top of the curtain box, see?" I said as I stood up, balancing myself on the sofa cushion to place the shiny penny out of sight on top of the curtain valance box. "There... now we will always remember that penny and be able to stop in time!" That pact lasted almost a year.

The movie I had been watching ended with the sound of loud wedding bells, which brought my consciousness back to the reality of my bedroom. I turned off the television, opened a new tablet to its first blank page, turned off the lights, and then drifted into a dreamworld filled with romance and weddings.

Five

One thing, all things: move among and
intermingle, without distinction.
To *live in this realization is to be*
without anxiety about non-perfection.

Chien-chih Seng-ts'an
Zen Patriarch, 606 AD

John Brackston stood tall beside his daughter, proud. His life had
not been an easy one, especially since his had wife died, leaving him
to raise Anna Jo alone. He was dressed in his long black coat with
white ruffled shirtsleeves spouting out the cuffs. He had saved the
clothes from his own wedding in Pennsylvania. His sandy blonde hair
lay flat against the back of his neck, thick with hair cream. His face
was shaven for the first time since the funeral of Anna Jo's mother
fifteen years earlier. On this day of his daughter's wedding, John's
German heritage ruled and he invited everyone he knew, and some he
did not, to witness the marriage between his daughter, Anna Jo, and
James.

Anna Jo waited for the signal from the minister to begin walking the
short path with her father. She had never felt so beautiful. Her wedding
dress was white silk and lace flowing to her feet, with a high neck
collar. June Livingston had sewn the gown with material from her own
wedding dress. Anna Jo had felt for many years that James' mother
was just like her own. After dressing in her cherished wedding dress,
Anna Jo accepted the gold chain with its silver heart from June. It hung
around her neck as she became Mrs. James Livingston.

The field was filled with people jumping up to see over the
shoulders of those in front as John walked Anna Jo down the dirt path

through the chapel's garden. He waved his free arm to everyone while holding tight his daughter's arm with the other. They arrived at the end of the path where James was also dressed in his best clothes of black shoes, a white shirt, black pants, and a newly seamed overcoat that touched his knees. June had worked for several weeks to complete James' coat for this special day. She was standing on the right side of the path, holding a handkerchief near her face to catch the tears she knew would well-up in her eyes. June was a fine lady, English as her husband had been. She had delicate features and dark hair wound up in a bun on her head with a silver pin to hold it in place. It was difficult for June to believe that ten years had passed since James first met Anna Jo. *Where did the time go?* she thought to herself.

When James saw Anna Jo coming toward him, he almost fell backward. He looked at the girl he always knew he would marry one day. He watched her as she looked around at all the people, and then their eyes locked. His face turned red and her cheeks flushed lightly. After Anna Jo's father placed her hand in his, James knew nothing could come between him and his love for her. The declarations were said and the handfasting was complete. Lawfully, they did not need their parents' approval, but they knew each of their single parents were very happy with the match. James kept Anna Jo's hand tight within his own as they laughed and danced well into the night to a mixture of English tunes and the hardy songs of Germany; and of course, beer was passed from hand to hand around the garden. Slipping out of the celebration, they made their way to the little cabin built for them to begin their life as husband and wife.

Living in the Virginia colony in the early 1700s was not an easy life. The division of labor and class was obvious. There were tobacco plantations owned by wealthy men who had many slaves to work the land. There were also many farmers who worked small farms and depended on local people to plant and harvest their crops without much pay except for the food they shared. Venturing to the American colonies was an adventure for everyone, especially the children. Schooling was usually a few lessons offered by a relative or friendly widow, hoping to receive a bit of money to help her sustain her solitary life. Mrs. Livingston was such a widow. She would sew, cook, teach children lessons, tend to animals, and even plant and harvest for farmers when she was needed. Being an independent woman, June vowed to do anything needed to raise her son to become well-educated like his father. Her efforts were not in vain, however; James wanted only to marry Anna Jo and secure his own land.

After a few years of tending other people's land and helping Anna Jo's father in the plantation stables, James wanted to travel west to find land of his own. He informed Anna Jo, "There was a fur trader that came into the stable today. He said he traveled south for about a thousand miles and found a break in the mountain range. He was then able to go west and saw a vast land untouched and ready for anyone who wanted to claim it. Anna Jo, I truly want to find our own land where we can farm just for ourselves and raise a family. Would you be willing to travel that journey with me?"

"Let's talk with Papa and your mother first, but it would be wonderful to have our own land! We could get help from others to build a house, I bet. Papa would give us a few horses and a wagon too. Oh, James, it does sound like a good idea!" exclaimed Anna Jo.

"Well, I'll talk with the fur trader and your pa tomorrow to find out when a good time would be to make such a journey. I hear that winter would not be a good time to go, so we have plenty of time to prepare," James said, showing signs of excitement in his face.

The two planned and talked about nothing else for weeks. They thought out how they would travel west to find land where they could farm and raise a family. Anna Jo was right about her father; he offered much of the necessary gear, in addition to the needed wagon and horses. On the other hand, June Livingston did not approve of the venture. Her memories of her husband leaving to travel west over the mountain range never to return were still painful to remember. She strongly argued against the move, but in the end, she lost to the eager couple who wanted a new life on their own. Finally, June resolved to help the young couple in any way she could. She began to save blankets, cloth, and cookware for them. She even made Anna Jo new dresses with heavy material that would hold up while sitting on the wagon's rough bench, or while riding a horse. June feared she would never see her son and his wife again, but she also knew her wish for them to stay near her was a dream only she possessed.

I closed Tablet #1 thinking how real the dream had been several nights ago. In many ways, it reminded me of David's and my early days together and how in love we had been. We had so much fun learning about new places to go when we were dating and newly married. My favorite places to visit were the beaches which were about an hour and a half west of where we lived. Since childhood, my family would rent a small house to spend a week or two at the beach during the summer months. My mother's family started the tradition when she and her siblings were young. Her mother and father would make the long trip through Carbon Canyon's winding roads to the ocean and stay with their three children in a little cottage near the shore. Mother told me once that she wished her father would have kept that little house so she could have passed it on to us. So David and I continued the tradition for our family, and we took our kids to the beach each summer to play in the sand and the ocean waves.

Once, before we were married, David wanted to drive up the California coastline and over to the town of Hollister where a national air show was being held. The trip would be the furthest we would go away from home, taking a full day and into the night for the entire round trip. I had to beg my father to let me go. He gave in when David came over to ask him and explained his strong desire to have me see the air show. David knew everything about airplanes. A few years earlier, when I saw his room for the first time, I had been awestruck to see all the airplane models hanging from the ceiling that he had made through his childhood years. David had gone through the AFROTC (Air Force Reserve Officer Training Corps) and was a Civil Air Patrol Cadet in high school and college. He became a licensed pilot too, but that is a whole other story!

We left before sunrise to take the scenic Highway 1 up the California coastline. We got to the air show in time to see the entire show, and then we went to meet some of the pilots and inspect their planes. We began our trip back home thinking we had plenty of time and would be back by about nine o'clock that evening. We even called my dad to let him know we were on our way home. Then we hit the famous California coastline fog. We couldn't see two feet in front of the windshield! It was dark when David pulled into the parking area of a small closed gasoline station. There was a phone booth beside the edge of road, so he called my dad a second time and explained it would not be safe to drive anymore that night. He came back to the car and told me we would need to sleep in the car until sunrise. Well, I was not afraid of the soupy thick fog, and I knew there were not any cars on the road to bring strange people to shine flashlights in the windows. My concern was... how would I ever be able to sleep with David so close to me? Neither of us slept very much that night.

Shaking my head to release the old memories, I entered my current reality and picked up Tablet #2. I settled into my reclining chair to continue reading the lifetime of James and Anna Jo....

രൂ

James asked the fur trader he had met in the stable which route would be best for them to journey alone. "Travel south first, along the mountain range from Virginia, then head west through those unknown territories until you find a place to settle," the burly man instructed. He told James it would not be a good idea to travel alone, but to wait for a wagon party to join. James was determined to leave that spring and not wait around until he heard there were others wanting to head west. So Anna Jo and James headed out alone together with their two horses and small wagon piled high with supplies and tools.

Sometimes there were no wagon trails in the dirt to follow, but James knew he could find a way around the large mountains named after the Alpalachee Indians who lived in the deep forests. Virginia settlers were used to seeing many different kinds of tribal Indians, and James learned a lot from them. Many of the Indians became slaves to the wealthy plantation owners, and when James had worked with his father-in-law in the stable, he learned some of the language and about the land west of the mountains. He knew when he found the right land to claim, he could rely on local natives to trade for supplies like salt to keep his game fresh. Although, there were stories of wild Indian tribes who terrorized settlers and even killed innocent families, James did not tell Anna Jo about those stories.

James and Anna Jo continued their journey southward until the mountains became hills and they could not take their wagon over them or through the deep valleys. They managed to arrive at a great river, which seemed impossible to cross. Then one night, a few traders joined them for supper and told them about the flat boat they could take to cross to the other side. They followed the instructions of going north until they came upon a type of levee manned by a hairy man who smelled like he had not taken a bath in months. He would take them on his flat boat to the opposite side of the river for a small fee. James had enough to pay the fee, and their wagon and two horses were set on the makeshift ferryboat. They all made it across.

The land was beginning to look a bit barren to James the further they traveled west. He had only known the hills of the Cumberland Mountains with their lush green trees and rich soil, but he was sure there was a perfect spot for them to settle, so he insisted they travel a bit further northwest. They arrived where a large river flowed easily into the great river they had crossed a few days earlier, and it was here

Cabin in the early 1700s

that both James and Anna Jo knew they had arrived at their homeland.

They set up a temporary campsite and shelter, knowing they would need their cabin to be built by winter. James worked each day from sun-up to sunset cutting down trees for the cabin. He was hoping a few other settlers would find them and pitch in to help, but no one came. After several months of building and planting the seeds Anna Jo had brought with her, they had a small garden and a cabin they could call their own, albeit, without a roof! James managed to make Anna Jo a hearth out of stones from the riverbank for cooking. And when the smoke from the little cabin's chimney filled the sky for a few days, nearby settlers searched them out and offered their help with raising the roof of their cabin. Soon, the property was realized just the way James had dreamed it.

James and Anna Jo became friends with the local Wichita Indians and felt safe with their gentle ways of living in their grass huts by the river's edge. Their villages were spaced along the river and they lived in round huts thatched with grass. James traded metal bowls and tools for salt blocks and skin hides. He heard sparse stories from the trappers of warrior Indians from the South and Southwest called Chickasaw. It was told that when they came upon settlers, they would destroy the farmland and, sometimes, even take young women as hostages. He did not tell Anna Jo any of this news when he returned from his hunting trips.

Anna Jo and James lived peacefully on their farm for several years. Then one day when they were tending their crops, a small band of Indians passed the outskirts of their land. James could see there were only a half-dozen young braves. These natives were not dressed the same, nor did they talk in the same language as their Indian friends by the river. They looked like Chickasaw from what James knew about the tribe. When they rode closer, James offered trading goods to the small party, but they shook their heads, grunted, and rode on.

As evening approached and James and Anna Jo sat down for supper, the little cabin door burst open to display the same young braves they had seen earlier. James noticed the difference in their appearance; they now had painted faces, and anger in their eyes. He rose to reach for his rifle hanging above the hearth when one of the warriors hit him on the side of the head. James fell to the floor, unconscious. Anna Jo stood straight and still as the Indians walked slowly around her, looking at her clothes and shoes, and then they began to laugh loudly. Anna Jo became angry and jumped for the rifle still hanging on the cabin wall, only to have a thick arm intervene and catch her in the neck. She too fell to the floor, near her beloved James. The young warriors, who were out riding for an innocent adventure, took the items they thought might bring rewards from their elders. One brave saw the small heart-shaped silver locket hanging around Anna Jo's neck and yanked it off... then they set the cabin on fire.

Six

When the mind exists undisturbed in the Way,
Nothing in the world can offend,
And when a thing can no longer offend,
It ceases to exist in the old way.

Chien-chih Seng-ts'an
Zen Patriarch, 606 AD

Many times through our years together, I suggested to David that I felt we had spent several lifetimes as Native Americans. When I attended graduate school in the 1980s, I took a class taught by Starhawk, the author of several insightful books on the topics of ritual traditions and ancient religions.

The class I took was filled to capacity. Eager to learn the ways of the indigenous people I knew I had been one of in previous lifetimes, I read Starhawk's book with awe and a personal sense of understanding. The class participated in sessions of drumming, dancing, chanting, throwing of stones, and many other rituals. For the final project, the students were instructed to separate into groups. Using the knowledge we had obtained, each group was asked to construct an authentic Medicine Wheel and then present the ceremony to the class. This sacred ritual came easily to me, as if I had performed it my entire life.

A Medicine Wheel is used for many occasions; one tradition is for healing the Earth and its population. The energies of all living creatures, Mother Earth, Father Sky, Grandfather Sun, Grandmother Moon, and the Great Spirit Wakan Tanka are called upon to be present. It is a ceremony to recognize and honor all life with gratitude. The ritual invokes the four corners, or directions of the Earth, as well as the four elements: wind, water, land, and sky.

Bighorn Medicine Wheel (Wyoming)

Objects such as stones, feathers, crystals, and animal totems are placed evenly at these points and in other locations within the circle, or wheel. Sticks of dried sage are burned, allowing the smoke to welcome and purify each direction and the wheel's participants.

I have always respected my deep connection to my Native American lifetimes. I honor the sky, wind, water, and Earth and all living creatures upon it. My animal totems are always near, guiding my way each day. This year, my power animal totem was chosen as the great Eagle, one who channels the energy of the Holy Spirit. Eagle energy brings the ability to live in the realm of the spirit world and yet remain balanced upon the Earth. As described in the book *Medicine Cards* by Jamie Sams and David Carson, "Eagle medicine is the power of the Great Spirit, the connection to the Divine." My connecting with Eagle power was an affirming *permission message* for me that the time was right to share the channeling that I received from David. Much of this communication has been detailed within the lifetimes we experienced together that I have shared in this book. The identifications of these lifetimes are listed at the end of this book in the "Lifetime Identification Chart" and "David's Story of Heaven," which I channeled from David's words.

A few days after Rich passed to the other side, I received from the

Holy Spirit another affirmation that I have lived one distinct Native American lifetime. I was sitting outside on the back deck and asking the air in front of me multiple questions about why our son needed to leave his life so early. I began to cry, and the crying progressed into sobs, and the sobs became sounds from deep within my soul. I sang the sounds over and over as if I could not stop myself from emitting them. Finally, exhausted from chanting, I stopped. I went to find David and repeated the tune to him, and then I asked, "Doesn't this sound like some sort of a tribal chant?"

"Yes, it really does," David replied.

"I wonder how I can find out if it is, or if Rich sent it to me from the other side?" I asked, knowing David had no answer.

A few months later, I was asked by a friend to participate in a healing Medicine Wheel ritual. She explained it would be in the mountains north of where I live and would be conducted by Sage Runningbear, a local shaman from the Pomo Nation. The Pomo tribe settled along California's Mendocino coastline and inland into Lake County. The Pomo are a peaceful people who perfected the art of basket weaving. I accepted my friend's invitation, and on the night of a full moon, I found myself completing a circle of women and listening to stories of past suffering. At the close of the ceremony, we stood and howled like wolves to the moon, and the healing was sealed. As we were leaving the wooded area, I walked beside Sage. I asked her if she would listen to the tune which I felt was sent by my son who had passed away a few months earlier.

"Yes, of course, Barbara. Do you have a recording of it for me to hear?" Sage asked.

"No, I don't have a recording, but that's a good idea! I will put it on my cell phone so I will always be able to listen to it. I can sing it to you now, if that's okay?" I asked as we walked to our cars.

"Yes, let me hear it," Sage affirmed.

I started singing the tune I knew so well and had sung many times on my daily walks just to feel the rhythm of the notes. When I had performed the chant a few times, I stopped to listen to what Sage might tell me.

"That is a Lakota mourning song, Barbara," Sage told me, with no element of surprise in her voice.

"Oh, you recognize it! Do you think Rich sent it to me, to comfort me?" I asked.

"You, Rich, and David were Lakota in a lifetime together Barbara.

You were one of the mourning women who went from tent to tent after the passing of a tribal member. The women would sit for hours chanting the same words over and over in deep guttural tones which could be heard for miles. You will learn of this lifetime one day, Barbara," Sage informed me.

Sage was correct. I did learn of this lifetime, through David's channeling.

❧

"Dear husband, why must you be gone for so many moons to fight and kill our brother nations?" asked Hawk Spirit.

"You must be patient my wife, soon we will have the perfect land on which to live," Rides with Wind replied, hushing his partner with a loving hug.

Hawk Spirit lived a hard life in the ways of the Lakota. Her once black hair, now streaked with grey, was tied in braids that hugged her breasts. Ten babies she had bore, each a child of one husband, Rides with Wind. He stood tall against his horse who took him away each year for months at a time to fight for the Lakota land. The Lakota's current enemy was the Cheyenne who lived in the Black Hills of the Dakotas. Once the land of the Kiowa Nation, the Cheyenne fought to take the hills for their own, now they would be challenged by the Lakota.

Hawk Spirit walked each day, with young ones by her side and her youngest on her back, to fetch the water from the wide river below their camp. The male children playfully mocked their warrior fathers who left the camp with their painted horses to defend their land. They jumped and ran as if they are riding their own horses into a fierce warrior's battle. Hawk Spirit reluctantly accepted that her people must fight for the land on which they lived; but, her ways were of brotherhood and peace, not battles leaving trails of blood for the vultures and wolves.

For as long as the sun has risen, the Lakota have lived with nature's cycles on the land of their fathers. Rides with Wind, son of Chief Black Feather, grew up strong in the beliefs of the Lakota. He learned early how to form the arrowhead spears and metal knives to take into battle. As all young boys did, he walked the vision quest and danced in the traditional sun dance ritual for twelve moons feeling the pain from his self-inflicted wounds. The Lakota are a very spiritual people, following

Lakota Oglala girl (John C.H. Grabill, 1891)

many rituals to ensure Wakan Tanka, the Great Spirit, is pleased with their journey.

When the Lakota ruled and tepees were spread throughout the land, fighting still commanded their lives. For a warrior, fighting a battle was as prestigious as having many children. Each victory brought more honor to a family and secured a higher ranking to enter the circle of chiefs. Rides with Wind wanted with all his heart to become Chief Rides with Wind. Hawk Spirit knew this desire when she met Rides with Wind and accepted the ways of her fathers, but her desires were far from the bloodshed of fighting. As a young girl, she grew up learning the ways of healing and bringing life into the world, and she did not feel honor in taking it.

Hawk Spirit was the daughter of Chief Elk Foot and Gentle Rain, the medicine woman of the Oglala Lakota who lived in the East. Hawk Spirit learned of the birthing, healing, and mourning rituals from her mother until she was old enough to complete them alone. When she met Rides with Wind, Hawk Spirit had been taken to a circle of Lakota west of her own to assist in the birthing of a great chief's twelfth child. Wakamisha, the children, are most sacred to the Lakota and every effort is made for a healthy birth and happy childhood. When Rides with Wind and Hawk Spirit's eyes met, they knew the bond would be sealed. They married soon after their first meeting with the blessings of their elders. It is tradition that the new husband move into his woman's family tepee; however, this time Hawk Spirit's entire circle moved west and the two circles joined, forming one of the largest tribes of the Lakota Nation. The Lakota tradition also includes that of monogamy, although a warrior brave could take a second wife if he desired. Rides with Wind did not choose a second wife, but lived happy with Hawk Spirit his entire life.

"*Ai*, I will sing the song of mourning again soon I fear," Hawk Spirit continued telling her husband.

"Let us pray to Wakan Tanka we will all be returning to those we cherish, and then we will pack and make the journey to our new land in the great hills," replied Rides with Wind.

"Will this be your last battle, dear husband?" she asked with hope in her voice.

"*Hin*, I will always be ready for fighting for Lakota land. Do not worry; your children will not lose their father soon," he said, bringing his wife close to his heart once again.

"I will ready your things," Hawk Spirit said, knowing she could say nothing further to her brave husband to stop him from pursuing his honor.

❧

It was 1776 in the White Man's Earth calendar when the Lakota warriors rode east to the Paha Sapa mountain range to fight for its land. Chief Standing Bear first discovered the Paha Sapa ten years earlier and talked of the day when the Lakota would defeat the Cheyenne and settle in the hills as their home forever. He named the hills Paha Sapa, the Black Hills, because when he saw the rolling hills for the first time, they looked black from the sun's shadow upon the abundant trees.

Hawk Spirit's youngest child, barely two years old, was named Little Foot. He was the last of Rides with Wind's children and the most cherished. He was born early and was as small as the river fish. His feet were half the size of his father's little finger, and was so named. He was lighter in skin, with deep penetrating eyes that held many mysteries. Sometimes in his sleep, Little Foot laughed out loud to his dream visions. Hawk Spirit would teach him the ways of birthing, which she had mastered through the years, bringing hundreds of souls into their life. Hawk Spirit knew Little Foot would one day be a sought after shaman with much healing knowledge given to him by the Great Mystery.

Rides with Wind left before the sun rose over the plains with the other warriors. They rode fast to reach their destination and rested at the base of the Paha Sapa to regain strength for the battle set with the Cheyenne. Rides with Wind thought he would surely become a chief after their victory. After two moons resting their horses and before the next sunrise, the warriors silently approached the natives living in the hills. But their surprise attack was met with readied warriors who had been secretly watching the party at the foot of the majestic hills. The fight was fierce and bloody, leaving only the old, children, women, and a few Cheyenne braves to surrender. They journeyed west out of the Paha Sapa to lower plain lands to make camp. Rides with Wind was wounded that day and was returned to Hawk Spirit's side. She used all her *pejula* medicine, but she could not keep her beloved husband alive.

For thirty days and thirty nights, Hawk Spirit sang her mourning song, which echoed through the plains. Her heart was broken, but she had to be strong for the journey to settle in the Paha Sapa would be soon. Hawk Spirit traveled with dignity and pride along with her people and her ten children to settle in the Black Hills. She taught Little

Foot all she knew of healing, birthing, and mourning the dead. He grew to be a great shaman, holding rituals for the Lakota of the Paha Sapa.

Earth Prayer

Grandfather, Great Spirit,
once more behold me on earth
and lean to hear my feeble voice.
You lived first, and you are older than all need,
older than all prayer. All things belong to you—
the two-legged, the four-legged, the wings of the air,
and all green things that live.
You have set the powers of the four quarters
of the earth to cross each other.
You have made me cross the good road and road of
difficulties, and where they cross, the place is holy.
Day in, day out, forevermore, you are the life of things.
~ Black Elk: Holy Man of the Oglala Lakota Sioux

I set Tablet #6 back on the night table to rest my eyes. Writing my memories from the deep meditation revealed new insight into how all our lifetimes intersect and reflect our soul's experiences. There does seem to be a true karmic effect unfolding concurrently between our lifetimes. In David's words that I had channeled:

All incarnated forms and souls have the seeds of knowing the laws of karma. It is up to them individually to learn and understand their karmic patterns in which to learn, grow, and evolve. Karma is a magical element of learning, growing, and evolving with the Oneness....

My mother was a closet reincarnationist. She was raised in a very religious family; her grandfather was a minister. I think this strict childhood instigated her seeking new belief systems and ways of thinking when she became an adult. She would tell my sisters and me that we could explore and choose to believe in whatever spiritual systems we wished. We all took advantage of her suggestion. During our teen years, we each asked our mother questions about her beliefs and she would state them simply. Her answers were always followed by her saying, "But you experience what you want and feel what is right for you. You do not have to believe the way I do." I have greatly appreciated growing up with this openness and acceptance of all religions and spiritual beliefs. My mother studied her own childhood Protestant beliefs, as well as other avenues of spirituality, such as Theosophy, The Rosicrucian Order, the writings of Edgar Cayce, Eastern philosophy, and Metaphysics. She formed a broad view of religious and spiritual beliefs. I followed in her footsteps, adopting a very eclectic spiritual belief system.

After staying home with my children while they were young, I yearned to continue my education and soon entered a local junior college, taking courses at night. Looking back on my life at that time, I see an eager young woman blessed with everything she had asked for: A loving hardworking husband, healthy children, the support of her family, and a beautiful custom-built home. But there was a lack or void in my life that I learned to fill by furthering my education. I received a full scholarship to the prestigious Pitzer College and continued my undergraduate studies. At the same time, I secured a position as head counselor and community educator at a new women's medical clinic. This decision changed my life.

The year was 1976, just three years post the Roe vs. Wade ruling that allowed pregnancy terminations to be performed legally in states voting to do so. We lived in California, one of the states that developed and passed the bill for women to obtain a legal abortion, even without parental consent, starting at thirteen years old. Representing the women's clinic, I went into the surrounding communities, giving lectures to high school and college students, women's groups, and various organizations as to the choices women had regarding an unwanted pregnancy since the Supreme Court ruling had passed. I also counseled and supported hundreds of women whose choice was to terminate their pregnancies. My experiences in those five years urged me toward pursuing my graduate and post-graduate degrees in the direction of counseling.

During those years of lecturing, counseling, and holding the hands of girls and women while they underwent their procedures, my spiritual beliefs became very clear to me surrounding birth, death, and afterlife. My role in the abortions I attended was only to comfort and console each woman by easing her emotional pain, never to sway or judge her decision. I knew personally how devastating it could be to find yourself with an unwanted pregnancy, it almost happened to us. Just three months after Cindy was born, I thought I was pregnant again. At that time, my life was a bit crazy trying to take care of our two babies. I was terrified when I entered my doctor's office. Thankfully, I was not pregnant, because the year was 1970 and abortions were still illegal in the United States. Now, as I reflect on my Atlantian and Lakota lifetimes as women who brought souls into their Earth life, I can understand the karmic balance of my assisting those desperate women in the 1970s.

Seven

For the unified mind in accord with the Way
all self-centered straining ceases.
Troubles and irresolutions vanish
and life in true faith is possible.

Chien-chih Seng-ts'an
Zen Patriarch, 606 AD

"Oh, Mia! I get more afraid every time I go too far from our home. I am afraid the crazy men on their horses are coming closer!" Kya announced to her sister.

"Yes, I know dear sister. We must stay close to be safe from harm," Mia answered as she turned to tie Kya's long hair into a bun to rest at the nape of her neck.

"Let us listen tonight as Mother and Father talk again of the crazy men on their horses and how they have ridden near. Perhaps we will learn more of their ways," Kya instructed as if she were the older sister.

"Yes, dear sister, we must learn all we can to be ready for the day when we might see these strange warriors," Mia explained, finishing her duty of caring for her younger sister's hair and clothing.

The sisters were happy living on the inner high plains of the great peninsula encompassed by many seas. They had studied with their mother the land and its location between the seas and where the different tribes made their civilizations. Their father had even taken the pair on a long journey to venture to the North to view the dark cold sea with its high cliffs and splashing waves. They were delighted to see the massive waters. The sisters were of Greek heritage and were fair in complexion with light brown hair. Mia was the eldest and stood taller than her mother. She had developed early as a young woman, for her fourteen years. Kya was of delicate features and Mia felt her sister was an angel and cherished her dearly.

Being born in Asia Minor (Anatolia) about 300 BC was not a peaceful time for the land, or anyone who lived upon it. Throughout the Hellenistic territory there was fighting by many tribes to claim as much land as possible to obtain its bounties, such as iron ore and other precious metals; as well as, to seize its people to be of service to their conquerors. There were tales being told of men with chariots pulled by horses, men wearing gold helmets carrying metal shields, and even severed heads strapped to the necks of their horses! Many nights when the sisters were supposed to be sleeping, they would secretly listen to those who gathered with their parents to share their stories of fighting and bloodshed. They heard their warnings to keep the women and children close for fear of them being taken by the warriors, never to return.

After one night of terrorizing tales, Kya and Mia could not sleep. They kept their eyes open well into the night. Mia whispered the next morning, "Dear sister, we must stay close, near each other, never letting a distance come between us!"

"Yes, I will stay at your side no matter what happens. Should we tell Mana that we know about the warriors?" Kya asked her sister.

"I would think that a good idea. Let us go find her as soon as we mind the goats," Mia responded.

Finding their mother preparing the morning food, Mia spoke up bravely, "Mana, what can we do if the wild warriors with metal hats come to our land?"

"How do you know of these men?" asked the sisters' mother.

"We have listened to the words of the gatherings in the night. Is it true the crazy horsemen will come to take our land?" Mia asked with terror in her eyes.

"Oh dear child, you must listen to my words. To be safe, you must always walk the land together, close side-by-side. Do you understand me?" she asked her daughters, looking at one and then the other.

"Yes, Mana, we will do as you say," Kya softly spoke.

"Ay, Mana, what if we see the crazy men? What do we do?" Mia demanded more instruction.

"Listen close my dear ones," their mother lowered her tone bending near her daughters' faces. "If you are ever deathly afraid when the warriors come close, drink this potion." Their mother took a small vial filled with red liquid from a fold in her clothing that was wrapped around her breast. She gave it to Kya to keep close to her heart under her clothing which was also wrapped tightly around her chest. "Mind you... *this will only be used if you fear for your life!*"

"Ay, Mana, we understand your instruction. Let us always be close to our home, so we are safe," Kya said, then patted the little fold of her clothing which only the three knew of its making.

As the weeks passed, it seemed the tales of fighting did not spread and many believed their land was safe. One day when the sun was warm, Mia and Kya wanted to walk the path to the nearby river to play in the cool water. They asked their mother if they could go and she agreed, telling them they must return home before sunset. Kya and Mia dressed comfortably in loose clothing, and tied their hair high on their heads. They tucked a few pieces of bread, a chunk of cheese, and a pot of honey into a pouch to be worn by Mia. Kya would carry the small water sheath. Lastly, the sisters kneeled in front of the family altar to ask the gods for protection on their journey.

"Did you hear the others talk last evening, Mia?" Kya asked with her green eyes widening as they walked along the path.

"Not everything; my eyes did not stay open the entire night. What did you hear, dear sister?" Mia asked, as she tugged at the leather binding holding the pouch in place at her side.

"Well, firstly... I listened to hear more of the warriors. I heard that the men are very dark, hairy, and stout. And, that they hold armor of metal and have long swords which they use to slash off the heads of their enemies! Sometimes, they strap the victorious display on their horse's neck to show how brave they have been! Oh, Mia... what manner of fighting this must be!" Kya exclaimed.

"What else did you hear?" Mia asked with eager anticipation.

"I think they are named Celts... or something like that. Many men talked over each other and it was most difficult to understand. But I know I heard that this tribe also has many gods. How could they have many gods and still be so hedonistic? Don't they follow their gods' bidding?" Kya asked her sister, knowing she would have no answer to offer.

"I only know that here, in Anatolia, we are protected by our gods. Mana has told us how to pray each day to keep our safety and our rich land. I will always obey her and not allow others to sway my beliefs. What more did you hear in the night, Kya?" Mia asked, as she once again tugged at the pouch leather, which had tightened around her shoulder.

A band of Celtic warriors

"Oh, I know! I listened carefully and heard one man say our people were defeated recently by these Celtic warriors, and that they were moving west. Which way is West, Mia?" Kya asked.

"This way is west, the way we are walking away from our home. I know this because Father took us north, that way, to see the great sea, remember, Kya?" Mia asked her sister as she pointed to the North.

"Well, if we are going west and the warriors are going west, are they coming toward us? Or, are they going to the East?" asked Kya.

Mia stopped her walking and thought for several minutes as she turned her body back-and-forth, looking one way and then another. "It all depends on where the warriors are coming from," Mia said assuredly.

"Another word I have not heard before last night is Gallic. I don't know what this word means either, but it sounded like they were talking about the crazy warriors again. No matter. Whatever their names, we are safe, close to each other, Mia," Kya announced and hugged her older sister with a tight squeeze.

"Let's rest here for a short time and eat some cheese and bread. My feet are tied and the sun is getting hot." Mia motioned for Kya to follow her steps up the small berm to sit in the shade of a tree.

Mia and Kya were not aware of the band of Galatians riding fast and closer toward them. The warriors were outfitted in fighting dress, including their gold metal helmets with horse tails flying high. Their swords were long and sturdy for hacking at their enemy's bodies. This raiding party was traveling as far West as it could go to claim the land as Galatia territory. After riding at top speed, the men slowed to rest their weary horses. The warriors slowed their pace even more when they came upon the two sisters who were continuing their journey, and then the warriors stopped.

"You there! Come closer," the robust warrior shouted to the two sisters. He rode high on his horse with his decorated shield held tight on the side of his steed. There were at least several dozen others riding behind him as he slowed to a stop to gesture toward Kya and Mia, instructing them to come near. He must have been the high leader of the band for his attire was decorated in gold and silver, including his dome-shaped helmet with horns on the top. His black beard was long and streaked with gray, and his eyes looked like piercing holes of molten iron. The sisters hesitated to approach the warrior, and he shouted again, "Are you both deaf? I said, 'Come near me!'"

Kya and Mia bowed down on their knees, placing their foreheads to the ground. Their motion was instinctual as a form of submission and honor. Neither girl wanted to speak, nor move from her kneeling spot. The sisters heard the other warriors begin to laugh loudly, and with this commotion, the leader shouted, "You will do as I say or your heads will be tethered to my horse!"

Mia looked up to see the secured sword being drawn and jumped up quickly, pulling Kya with her to a standing position. Slowly, Mia guided Kya beside her as they stood in front of the wheezing horse.

"What is it you wish?" Mia bravely managed to ask.

"Ha! What do you think, young woman?" he laughed loudly. The rest of the warriors also laughed and jeered at the two young girls.

"We want to do no harm; let us pass to continue our journey to the river. We have nothing to give you," Mia spoke up a second time.

"And you, there, the shorter one. Do you not have anything to give me?" the warrior asked Kya.

"No sir. I have nothing," Kya softly replied.

"Well, I think different!" shouted the leader as he glanced around to the other warriors, smiling broadly. "You have no coins to give me?" he inquired.

"No sir. We are too young to accept coins," Mia explained.

The head warrior reached down into his pouch, hanging from the stag's neck, and with a flick of his wrist, he threw a few silver coins to land at the sisters' feet. "There, now you have coins to give me! Pick them up and bring them to me," he commanded.

The sisters stood rooted to the ground.

Frustration settled in the warrior's red face as he announced to his flank, "I want that one!" His long fat finger pointed to Kya.

Kya looked deep into Mia's loving eyes for direction, but she found none. Very softly, she whispered, "Mia, *I fear for my life.*" Quickly, she found the vial she had been carrying close to her heart for so many days.

"Noooo, Kya! You must not..." Mia's words struck silence as she grasped for the vial, only to obtain it empty. Kya dropped limp to the ground and Mia's legs fell beneath her. Mia's tears fell upon her sister's peaceful face. She raised her head and her wide eyes found the old warrior's face as she decreed, "This girl's spirit will haunt you forever."

When I channeled David's words about the lifetime of the two sisters in Asia, I instantly knew mine and Rich's soul had experienced that tragic life together. When I learned of Kya's death, I felt a deep soul loss as if a part of my life had also died, just like when Rich died. I felt touches of guilt when our son died, even knowing we had done everything we could to guide Rich to sobriety and help him deal with his painful back injury. Reading about the bond these sisters had and how devastating it was for Mia to lose her sister, I once again felt all the emotions of losing Rich. It was as if my soul again felt the pain of not being able to save the one I loved so dearly.

Even if we feel strongly that there is an afterlife, we search for comforting answers when someone we love moves into it. In some philosophies, the afterlife is considered far more idyllic than a mere life upon the planet. The material plane is thought to be only a base level of existence. The other side, or afterlife, is considered the true essence of a soul's being. I believe there are as many philosophies about life and death as there are people on Earth. When David and I talked about religion and spiritual beliefs, we usually had many similar concepts—sometimes, just a different vocabulary to describe them.

About a year and a half after David died, I found a hardbound diary among his things. I opened it to read "The Standard Diary for 1958" Property of David Sinor. I was amazed that he had not shared this journal with me. He would have been sixteen years old when he wrote in this diary for an entire year about his young life. The timeline would have been three years before we met. It took me several days to read through every word of the 365 pages written with a brown ink pen. I read his entries about his high school classes, and his needing to raise money to buy his uniform for the local Civil Air Patrol Cadets (An Auxiliary of the United States Air Force) and the ROTC (Regional Officer Training Corps) to which he belonged.

In his diary, I read about David's adventures frog hunting at Prado Dam with the boys I eventually met, and about the time he bought his first car. Also, entered on each Sunday were his studies in Sunday School. I had not even known he went to Sunday School as a boy! There was even a little black and white photograph tucked between the pages on the Sunday he graduated from his Sunday School Class that year. In the photograph, he stood first on the left of a row of boys, all several inches taller than him. David may have been shorter than all his classmates, but his body housed a big heart and compassionate soul.

After we had been going together for about one year, David told me he wanted to join the Air Force Academy and become a pilot. He had already obtained his pilot's license and even taken me up in a small Cessna airplane a few times.

Cessna 175 (1960)

In his diary, David also wrote down every book he had purchased or checked out of the local library that year—they all had something to do with flying! He sounded especially passionate about one book titled, *God is My Co-Pilot*, written in 1943 by Colonel Robert L. Scott, Jr. I looked it up on the Internet and found the classic book, which begins with the author dreaming of flying at age twelve years old. That book must have made a lasting impression on David's own dream to become a pilot. The only other item that was placed between the pages of his diary was a yellowed newspaper clipping of a large black rocket ship with several people standing around it. The caption read: "BLACK BEAUTY This is North American Aviation Co.'s rocket space ship, the X-15 which may make the first manned trip into space. It will make a test flight in February." The date on the back of the clipping read 1956.

With David's passion for flying and his sharing of his desire to join the Air Force, I was not surprised when he told me, about a year after we had met, that he had been undergoing the necessary tests to join the United States Air Force Academy in Colorado to be trained as a pilot. At the time, I did not ask more questions or get the details of his plans; after all, I was only sixteen when he shared this goal with me, and I really had no idea what it meant. As I sorted through more of David's boxes after he died, I was amazed at my discovery! In a neat stack of envelopes, I found letters addressed to David from the California Senator and the Vice President of the United States at that time, Lyndon B. Johnson. The letters detailed the written, verbal, and physical testing he went through to be considered as a cadet in the United States Air Force Academy, and that he had met all but one requirement.

I will always remember the day David came to my house and told me how disappointed he was that he had been accepted by the United States Military Academy at West Point to be trained as a navigator, not a pilot. His eyes were red as he explained he had passed all the testing, but was found to be one inch too short to be trained as a pilot. Then he defiantly stated, "So, I am not joining the service." I cannot imagine how our lives would have changed if he had accepted the appointment to West Point.

Eight

*Truth is beyond extension or
diminution in time or space;
In it a single thought is ten thousand years.*

Chien-chih Seng-ts'an
Zen Patriarch, 606AD

"You will be a man soon, my son. I give to you a wife this day," Tolui's father announced. Tolui had always been the favorite son; he was the youngest of four between Temujin and Borte. Tolui also had many half-siblings, for his father had many consorts, but Borte was Temujin's primary wife since the age of twelve. Tolui was the smallest of the brothers, but he held a strong bow and formidable stance upon his horse. His father's gift came when he turned eleven years old, as twelve was the age a young man could marry.

"Thank you, Father," the young Tolui replied and bowed from his waist in respect. Tolui knew his father was a great chieftain winning many battles. He himself would enter his first combat after his training. His young life was filled with learning to ride swiftly, to perfect the bow given him five years prior, and to study the tactics of obtaining victory for his people.

When Tolui was seventeen, his wife, Sorghaghtani, gave birth to his first son. The occasion was celebrated through the great territory, which expanded yearly from the Black Sea to the Atlantian Ocean. Temujin was known as the Ruler of the Mongol Empire, conquering most of the territory riding with his hundreds of thousands of warriors. Tolui was too young to go into battle with his father who traveled to the far ends of the land, but he studied hard through the years to gain

Mongolian Yurt

the approval of the Great Khan. He learned well from his father how to lead the enemy into battle, and then use the strong bows to attack with surprise. When he became twenty-one, Tolui was sent into combat and returned victorious, pleasing Temujin. Soon, Tolui was given his own men to lead into battle and traveled throughout the land.

"You are strong, my husband; I will be with you always," Sorghaghtani told Tolui. They lived among the people in simple huts or yurts, which made it easier to be near current battles. The Mongols were a strong, spirited group of people who followed their chieftain from birth to death as they roamed the deserts and nearby hills.

"I must go this day, as my father has instructed, to Nishapur and Merv. I am to be the head chief to take the land for our own," Tolui announced, standing taller than usual. "I will obey our Great Khan and become the chief he desires of me."

"Yes, you must go do this, my husband. I will wait for your return."

Tolui left that day to ride west into Nishapur with ten thousand horsemen. The date was 1221 AD and there was revenge in the air, for the husband of Tolui's sister was killed in an earlier revolt. The Great Khan ordered all inhabitants be killed. Tolui followed the orders, pressed further into Merv, and ordered more tribes massacred, including women and children. When he returned, Tolui earned the honor of his father and his tribesmen.

Soon, the mighty Mongols knew no foe. They had conquered such a mass of territory that they were feared by all, stretching from sea to sea. Tolui's father, Temujin, became known as the Universal Ruler, or Genghis Khan. When Temujin turned sixty-five years old, he had to decide who would be his successor; he had four sons who could be eligible to continue his honor.

"Wife, Father will soon choose who will be Chieftain of the Mongols. I am ready if I am his choice, but I believe my brother would be the better khan. Will you be disappointed if I am not chosen?" Tolui asked his wife.

"Your rule will come in time, dear husband. You have fought hard and strong for Temujin; that is your destiny," Sorghaghtani responded.

"Yes. My turn will surely come to rule," Tolui affirmed.

ॐ

Mongolian Warriors

"Come, Tolui; we will go to battle and become victorious over the Khwarezmian Empire and claim it for our own. The shah has betrayed us and a massacre of our people has transpired. Alert your army of my plans. We will combine our men with the two bands led by your brothers to present a full stance. We ride in twelve days," Temujin shared with his son.

"Yes, Father. I will obey your orders," replied Tolui.

Later the next day, Tolui asked his wife, "What is your feeling about the state of my father going, yet again, into combat?"

"His body is weakening. He must not ride to the front, but observe from behind. This is the vision I see, dear husband," she offered.

"I feel this also, but who shall tell him? Not I," Tolui said, shaking his head as he went to prepare his weapons.

In the great battle of 1227 to overthrow Khwarezmia, the Great Khan was wounded and soon died, leaving his kingdom to his youngest son, Tolui. This was decreed until a formal count could be made for the ruler's successor. Tolui had maintained the greater and more powerful army over any of his brothers; therefore, he commanded over the Mongol Empire for the two-year interim. Once the tally was made of the people, the title of chieftain was given to Tolui's next oldest brother. Later, when Tolui's brother became ill and the shamans recommended a sacrifice be made to kill the evil that had entered their ruler, Tolui volunteered to drink the poison. He died for the sake of his people by saving his brother, the Khan and Emperor of the Mongol Empire.

❧

In the middle of the night, the wind and rainstorm tumbled a chair on the deck outside my bedroom. I curled down deeper into the covers with my eyes open, listening to the torments of nature. Soon, my own tormented memories demanded reflection as I thought about David's and my divorce. When Richie and Cindy were twelve and ten years old, David and I had a few brief separations, thinking we could resolve our relationship differences by using the distance-makes-the-heart-grow-fonder technique. We were wrong. We sat through six months of couple's counseling, only to arrive at our decision in 1980 to divorce amicably. I moved into a nearby house so the kids could attend the same schools, and they alternated their stays between us every two weeks. This arrangement was great for the kids, but it left David and me in limbo—not wanting to resume our relationship, but living too close to move forward with another.

Within a few years, I chose to move to northern California, where my younger sister, Paula, had moved a year earlier. After making one trip to scout out a place to rent, I returned to tell the kids we would be moving. Cindy came with me and Rich chose to stay with David so he could continue in his high school. My choice to move was a jump-into-the-void decision, for I moved without the security of employment. My angels were with me, however, and I found a position as the Administrative Assistant to the President of World College West, a small four-year liberal arts college tucked in the barracks of Fort Cronkhite on the ocean's edge in Sausalito. This position was a good start for me because I was able to learn about other universities in the area where I could pursue a master's degree.

Those years of raising Cindy, working for several different employers, traveling to exchange the kids with David, starting up a counseling practice, and going to college at night, were challenging to be sure. I needed to adopt that inner Mongol warrior persona that my soul had previously experienced in order to sustain my sanity. However, being on my own for the first time in my life also gave me a new sense of independence and accomplishment I had never known. There is definitely a plus in a young woman leaving her parents' house to live on her own first, instead of directly marrying or moving in with a partner. This time allows a young woman to find her own ground and realize individual goals before working with a partner to create mutual plans.

David and I met regularly those years we were apart, sometimes to exchange the kids for the summer months and holidays as most divorced couples do, but we also continued our intimacy and love for each other, which most divorced couples do not do. Soon, David was making trips north just to be with me and we renewed our relationship. He eventually moved permanently so we could live together, and we remarried in a loving ceremony in front of very happy friends and family.

I also needed to reach for my warrior-self during other experiences in my life, including the deaths of my parents, son, two dear friends, and finally, my husband. I believe we all possess that warrior within us who will answer the call to go to battle for our protection and/or freedom. I know at the time I had experienced sexual molestation as a child, I felt there was an inner sense of barriers being crossed, and it was my inner warrior who came to rescue and guide me to stand firm.

Needing to bring out that defending energy early in my life gave me a genuine sense of self-worth I would not have found otherwise. I believe without my soul's Mongol lifetime experience, I could not have overcome many of the challenges or achieved the accomplishments I did in my life. I feel blessed to have an inner warrior's spirit to draw upon as a source of strength to support me through my lessons in this lifetime.

ॐ

When I moved north, just over the famous Golden Gate Bridge spanning the gateway into San Francisco from the County of Marin, I felt like I had returned home. Driving through the rainbow tunnel to view a new world waiting for me, I felt an inner-knowing that haunted me. It was a sense of déjà vu that I had once experienced settling near a warm fireplace to gaze through windows at the ocean waves rolling over and over upon the sandy shoreline. Living in Marin in the 1980s was filled with new experiences and exciting trips to nearby places to taste the local wines, watch the beauty of a sunset over the bay, and hike along the lush green foothills below Mount Tamalpais. I was escorted into the city to view the American Ballet Company perform *Swan Lake* and to attend other cultural affairs. I especially loved going to the famous Tamalpais Mountain Plays, which were performed each summer. Cindy and I would either ride in the provided bus or with friends up the steep windy road. Sitting outside on a sunny day listening to the voices of a theater company sing and recite the script of *Carousel* or *The Wizard of Oz* was one of my favorite things to do with my daughter.

It was at this time that I chose to continue my education at John F. Kennedy University, which was then located in Orinda. The commute to JFKU from Marin County took about one hour, so I was one busy lady for the three years it took me to complete my master's degree. During those years of classes, reading, writing, and studying, my relationship with Cindy seemed to fade. She was doing her *thing* in high school, which was not unusual for someone her age, but we just misconnected somehow. In her junior year, she declared she wanted to move back down south to live with her father. My heart broke, but I wanted to support her and gave my permission, if David was all right with the move.

Cindy soon left and I moved into a house with my sister, Paula, and another friend. Since Paula was also attending JFKU, we could coordinate our classes and drive together most of the time, which really helped with expenses. After graduating, Paula and I celebrated by treating ourselves to a vacation in Hawaii. We had completed a joint master's thesis, and since we were living together, we used that opportunity to extend our writing into a book. *Beyond Words: A Lexicon of Metaphysical Thought* was my first published book and I felt elated! Paula and I have always felt we were male Russian dancers in a past lifetime; however, in David's channeling, that life was not revealed to me. I am sure Paula and I have had many other lifetimes together. Paula is an internationally renowned sculptor who currently lives just minutes from me.

Nancy, my older sister, is a retired professor of nursing and lives in southern California. We see each other as often as possible, usually when I go down to stay at my favorite beach in the summer. David's channeling acknowledged one lifetime with her, although I am sure there were others as well. My sisters have been the wind beneath my wings as the song goes, and I love them both dearly.

It was not a coincidence that my studies included that of human consciousness at JFKU, which spurred me toward experiencing deep meditations. It was during one of these meditations that another lifetime came to me in a lucid vision—I had lived in San Francisco in the early 1900s. My intuition would not allow me to push this lifetime about living in San Francisco during the 1906 earthquake from my mind.

Nine

If the eye never sleeps, All dreams will naturally cease.
To understand the mystery of this One essence
Is to be released from all entanglements.

Chien-chih Seng-ts'an
Zen Patriarch, 606AD

"Carrie, hurry or we will miss the trolley!" Carrie's mother urged.

"Yes, I am coming! I am so excited," Carrie exclaimed as she stepped down the staircase as fast as she could in her floor-length frock.

"Your father is so eager to show us the elegant establishment that has been rebuilt a few years past. We have tried to journey to view it, but the traveling has been inconvenient. Now, the trolley can take us most of the way. It is said that it looks like a huge chateau with several stories, peaks, and steeples! Hurry, Carrie, and watch your skirt that it does not dirty in the street," Carrie's mother warned.

Carrie's mother was a proper lady in every sense of the word. Her name was June Anna, although she preferred to be called Anna. Her large blue-gray eyes told of her English ancestors who had migrated to the Americas, claiming for her a heritage of prominence. Moving to San Francisco, the Evingtons enlisted their knowledge of the shipping industry to help establish its port of commerce. When Anna met the man she was to marry, she had barely turned twenty years old. The following year, in the spring of 1870, Anna became Mrs. Anna E. Williamson. Their daughter, Carrie Anna Williamson, was born a year later.

Carrie's father was a medical doctor, establishing a practice soon after completing his studies at the University of California in San

Francisco. John graduated with high honors and also became a Demonstrator of Anatomy Professor in the university's medical department. Carrie had always known her father wanted her to enter into the medical profession. All through her childhood, he would question her often on topics encompassing the body's mechanics and which known tincture or physicality might well be applied to a person.

"Come, dear; Father is waiting to take us to the appointed trolley stop for the journey," Anna signaled to her daughter with her black glove, which made its way halfway up her arm.

"I am ready, Mother," replied Carrie, looking prim in her green skirt with white lace tight at her bodice. "We shall have so much fun!"

John Williamson had become a hardy man after his weakening younger years. Currently, he sported a handsome beard and mustache. His attire was a brown tweed suit with matching top hat; rarely did John go out without his top hat. His light brown hair with narrow streaks of gray distinguished him as one of the well-known Englishmen of the era. John's family had come to the Americas when he was only two years old. He had suffered illness during the ship's journey on the high seas, but he had regained his health once his family settled on the eastern shores of the Americas. His father was an eager traveler and brought his young family West in the mid-1800s. They eventually settled in the burgeoning town of San Francisco.

Carrie and her mother's excitement could not be contained as they rode in their horse drawn buggy to the trolley stop. The trip would take most of the day to complete, but the two women were already feeling giddy. "What does it feel like to ride in a trolley, Father?" asked Carrie.

"It is a bumpy ride to be sure, but the view is most enjoyable," replied John as he waved to a passing associate walking in the opposite direction.

"Well, I surely hope the trolley ride is appropriate for women. John, there *are* women who sit on the trolley?" asked Anna of her husband.

"Yes, my dear. Do not worry... we are approaching the point to board, right over there," John said and pointed in the direction of a group of people standing near the steel rails wedged into the cobblestone street.

The three did not need to stand in the group but a few minutes before the trolley's loud crackling noise, from its metal wheels upon the rails, delivered it right in front of them. John took Anna's arm and helped her get settled on the wooden seat, then did the same for Carrie.

Cable car in San Francisco (1901)

The others boarded, taking their place either in the open-framed area, or the covered-carriage car. The trip would deposit the passengers closer to their destination, and then they would need to board another buggy to take them the remainder of the journey.

John had made this trip earlier with a friend to be certain his wife and daughter could handle the rigors of the journey. Once he had viewed the restored Cliff House, he knew Anna and Carrie must experience it. The original Cliff House had burned down a few years earlier, in 1894, but a new owner had rebuilt it in a majestic fashion. John was anxious to see the looks on his wife and daughter's faces when they arrived at the celebrated mansion.

As the buggy approached their destination, Carrie exclaimed, "Oh my, what a gorgeous sight!"

"John, will we be able to have our lunch here? This is very impressive!" Anna whispered to her husband.

"Oh, yes. I have it all set that we shall walk the grounds, have some luncheon, and watch the sea birds from the second floor balcony," responded John, fingering his beard.

The buggy pulled up to the entrance of the Cliff House and the family began their tour of the interior. There were rooms for eating, some for sitting to socialize, rooms just to gaze upon art pieces from local artists, several dance halls, and lounges for those with a desire to visit a drinking bar. Carrie and her mother were thoroughly impressed and gossiped readily to one another about the decor, choices of food offerings, and the beauty of the ocean views. That day, the Williamson family clearly experienced a special occasion to remember.

Sadly, in less than ten years, the famous Cliff House burnt down a second time, even after surviving the catastrophic earthquake of 1906.

It seemed like a lifetime ago that Carrie was a young university student, happy to be attending classes and studying to become a doctor. Her days were filled with laughter and friends. Now at twenty-seven years old, Carrie reflected on the stresses of her life several years prior. Three years ago, she had moved into her own loft, which suited her lifestyle. She was located just far enough from her parents' home to allow her the freedom she needed to pursue her own career direction. Carrie looked out the window high above the street, only to find herself beginning to feel absorbed in the view of foamy sea waves splashing the shoreline. She opened her eyes wide, as if to remove the hypnotic effect the ocean had on her consciousness, and continued to pen her letter.

Cliff House (1902)

Dear William,

   As I sit and watch the waves break upon the shore, my heart also breaks with thinking about you being so far away. I so wish I could hold your little hand in mine and listen to your playful words. I am sending you a picture card of the great chateau my papa took us to visit today. One day I will take you there too!

   Please be a good boy and do your studies, for then you will become a fine man and teach others what you have learned. I must go now, my darling, for the light is dim and my eyes are tired from a full day of pleasure.

   Remember, dear William, we will be together one day. I will take you to the shore, which you have never seen, to hear the sea birds and ocean waves that I love so dearly.

Your Aunt,
Carrie

Carrie neatly folded the letter with the picture card into an envelope, closed the desk secretary lid and stumbled to bed. Her mind drifted to the day William was born and tears fell upon her soft pillow. She turned on her side and drifted into a deep sleep.

It had always been evident to Carrie that she wanted to become a doctor like her father. She reveled in the thought of helping someone heal from an injury or illness. Her studies at the university were not as difficult for her as for the other students, for she had read and studied her father's books for several years prior to entering the university's medical program. When Carrie applied to enter the school, it had been only a few years earlier that the UCSF Medical School's Board decided to accept women into its prestigious program. Even now, her responsive answers to the professors' questions were many times received with looks of disdain. However, Carrie was determined to finish her studies and develop her own medical practice, focusing on women's medical needs and health.

One night as she was talking and laughing with her friends at a party celebrating the end of the year's lessons, Carrie glanced across the room to see a young man obviously staring at her. She kept her head motionless but smiled to display her approval, and immediately, the young man strode across the floor to her side.

"I was noticing your laughter and found my eyes unwilling to look away," stated the young man as he looked even deeper into Carrie's eyes.

"My name is Carrie Williamson, and yours may I ask?" Carrie questioned feeling a bit uncomfortable.

"No need to reveal my name just yet, my dear Carrie. We will know each other well, soon I feel," the young man retorted with a wide grinning smile.

"Well, are you a student in the medical studies?" Carrie asked, settling in a nearby chair.

"Yes, and you are the famous Carrie Williamson, daughter of Dr. John Williamson," he stated with assurance.

"Yes, I am. Do you know of my father?" Carrie questioned, trying desperately to learn more from this handsome young man.

"Everyone in university knows of the great Dr. Williamson! I have had studies in class with him just last year," he proclaimed with apparent arrogance.

"Well, then you must be end year…. Where will your practice be?" Carrie asked while she secured her hat tighter to her hair.

"I may travel east, but I have not really decided. The night is ending; would you take a walk in the night air with me, Carrie Williamson?" He stood and laughed as he bowed as if to portray an Englishman asking his lady to dance.

"I guess that would be fine, but just a short walk for I must be home soon or my parents will worry," Carrie offered as she stood beside the mysterious blue-eyed young man.

"Here, take my arm, young lady," he said, still pretending to play at his game of rescuing his damsel-in-distress.

"I can surely walk without your arm, sir," Carrie replied with a hint of displeasure in her voice.

"As you say, mi'lady," said the young man, lowering his outstretched arm.

As the couple walked outside through the courtyard, Carrie tried to decide whether she was fond her young suitor. There was certainly a curiosity within her as she felt her body's sensuality begin to awaken. After walking and chatting for quite some time, Carrie felt it was time to return to the company of the others and turned in that direction. She soon realized the young man had led her down through an unlighted area of the grounds with which she was unfamiliar.

"I believe we must return to the party; let us walk back toward it," Carrie said as she started up a small grassy incline.

"Oh no, not yet… do allow me to taste those rose-colored lips," he suggested as he lunged forward to kiss Carrie on the mouth. His kiss was long and hard, and without relent. At first, Carrie felt the urgency of his body and kissed him in return, only to sense quickly her inner doubts and she tried to push him away. Her resistance was met with more boldness and strength. He forced Carrie down on the grass, all the while pressing his body firmly to hold her tightly against him. Carrie believed she had fainted, and then realized he was inside her. As her awareness returned, she slapped her uninvited lover across the face. He rose to stand above her, only to laugh at her sprawled out below him. He offered his hand to pull her to her feet and Carrie slapped it too!

Carrie did not mention the forced indiscretion to anyone as she gathered herself together to join the others. The young man did not return to the party, and Carrie was left to deal with the guilt of the clandestine event alone. Before Carrie's next school term began, she knew she was pregnant. She waited a few months longer to tell her mother and father of her tormented evening walk and its current results. John and Anna were very upset, but they also knew their anger toward the young man was worthless compared to the pressing issue of supporting their daughter. Anna helped Carrie conceal her condition and suggested she return to her studies as if nothing had happened. Carrie's father told her that when the time was close for the impending birth, he would take her by train to the Midwest where his sister and her husband, Clara and Walter Muir, would tend to her needs.

Carrie obeyed her father's instructions and returned to her studies at the university. In each class, and at all the gatherings of students, she searched for the young man who had taken advantage of her, but he was never to be seen again. In the final stages of Carrie's pregnancy, she traveled with her father and mother to Missouri where the Muir family lived. There she was tended by her father and she gave birth to her son. Carrie fell in love with her son the moment he was placed in her arms to suckle. He had her fair complexion and light eyes, and a dimple in his chin. This dimple was the only defining mark possessed by little William that indicted there had been another person involved in his conception.

Following a month of recuperating and nursing William, Carrie knew her bond with her son would be forever. However, John and Anna had other plans for their daughter than raising a child out-of-wedlock and discontinuing her medical studies. Carrie's father told her that she must leave the baby to be cared for by the Muirs. She would take the train back to San Francisco to continue her schooling or she would never be the doctor she wanted to become. Anna was more hesitant in acknowledging her husband's wishes, but in the end, she also agreed this was the best plan. She even suggested that Clara and Walter give the baby their surname to legalize an adoption of her daughter's illegitimate child. This was done and little William became William Paxton Muir. Anna assured Carrie that in a few years, when the time was right, she could bring the child to live with them as a younger relative who had lost both of his parents.

Carrie was fraught with fear that she would never see her little boy again. The morning they left for the train station, she touched his tiny body and kissed the soft spot atop his head. She whispered in his ear that she would send for him soon. Her heart sank when the train pulled from the station, and she was silent the entire ride home. Carrie stayed in touch with Clara through letters, to obtain the newest updates regarding young William's life. Clara returned every letter, detailing William's latest methods of crawling, walking, and learning his first words. As the years passed and Carrie's desire to complete her medical studies came in second to her desire to secure her child near her, she moved out of her parents' home and into a small loft in the western area of the city.

In 1898, Carrie's life revolved around her chosen method of doctoring. She tended the surrounding neighborhood residents with her specialized medicinal healings by going to the homes of those ill or in need of directive medical advice. Her professional bag was filled with tinctures and herbs that she gladly shared, along with any instruction she learned from the university. Carrie did not complete her educational studies, but instead moved into a more nurturing and holistic method of healing, which felt very familiar. John and Anna accepted that their daughter's life would never meet their idealized expectations, and they loved her unconditionally. Carrie had taken this day from work to be with her parents, especially to please her father.

Victorian Era Women

Ten

The Way is beyond language,
for in it there is
no yesterday
no tomorrow
no today.

Chien-chih Seng-ts'an
Zen Patriarch, 606 AD

After David moved north to be with me in 1989, we took several small trips around the San Francisco area. We traveled north to the Napa Valley and into Calistoga to experience the warm climate, drink the local wines, and soak in the mineral baths heated by Mt. Helena's dormant lava beds. On one of our trips, we stayed overnight at a favorite spa to enjoy the relaxing sun and water. That evening while we were soaking in one of the hot pools, David turned to me and said, "I guess we better get married again."

"Is that a proposal?" I asked, looking deeply into his eyes for the answer.

"Yes, I guess it is," David said and held me close. We were married a second time the following year.

We took a wonderful honeymoon cruise along the California coast down into Mexico, stopping first at Catalina Island. We rode a small boat from the ship to Catalina's marina and thoroughly enjoyed walking around the island. We even watched the fish swim in the water beneath us while riding in the glass-bottom boat. The cruise was exactly what we needed, something to take us far away from our daily

Our 1991 Wedding; Paula, Barbara, and Nancy

Our 1994 Hawaii Vacation

lives in order to reconnect once again.

When we moved back to southern California a few years later, we were able to take another romantic vacation, this time to Hawaii. I had visited a few of the Hawaiian Islands without David, so I said, "If we're going to go, let's visit at least two of the islands. We could visit the Big Island and Kauai." I suggested Kauai because I had not been there and I had two girlfriends who lived on the island whom I wanted to visit. It was 1994 and my second book had just been published, so this trip was for celebrating! Every day, David would bring me a gorgeous wild flower to place in my hair... he was so romantic.

Again, being away together afforded us the time to reconnect and talk of our future plans. When we returned from the islands of paradise, we found anything but paradise waiting for us at home. Our son, Rich, had acted out during our absence and we were confronted with several more years of tug-o-war battles with his addictive behavior. I have written about many of those experiences in my book *Tales of Addiction and Inspiration for Recovery*, so I will not share the details again of those painful ten years. I also experienced many personal accomplishments during this time period, such as my next few books being published, completing my doctorate degree, and maintaining a successful counseling practice in southern California. I am not sure how I managed it all, but it was very rewarding to have followed through with my goals.

Also within those ten years, our daughter Cindy married, which made us very pleased and excited. David rented a big Lincoln sedan for us to make the trip up to Marin County where the wedding ceremony was to be held near Cindy's new home in Mill Valley. David walked Cindy down a steep garden staircase to present her to the man we learned to love as our son. About a year later, I was honored to be present when my grandson was born! I traveled north to stay with friends during Cindy's last few weeks of pregnancy, and I was able to stay another few days after the birth of our grandson. Every few months, David and I drove back up north just to hold little Jessie in our arms.

In 1998, David was injured while working and underwent two surgeries. It became evident that he would not be able to return to his profession of floor installation, so he soon retired. Rich had settled down somewhat, so David and I began talking about moving to northern California to be closer to Cindy and her family. These talks kept our dreams alive and the years rolled by quickly. By about 2002, I was also ready to retire from my counseling practice and our plans began to manifest each time we traveled north. During our trips, we would scout out the different towns in Marin, Sonoma, and Napa Counties, then as far north as Lake County, where my sister Paula and her husband had moved. We eventually fell in love with the little community of Hidden Valley Lake. The area was near Cindy, yet far enough away for us not to encroach on her growing family.

Now, as I reread my channeled words from Tablet #9, I am left with a vague sense of knowing. I pressed the tablet to my breast, hoping to feel a return of David's energy, which had been channeled so freely. Eager to capture his essence again, I retrieved Tablet #10.

"John, is that you coughing?" asked Anna.

"Yes, dear. I am afraid my patients this week have gotten the best of me," John replied as he coughed once again. He searched for the vial labeled tincture of iodine within his black medicine bag. John hated to be ill; it reminded him of his childhood and why he pursued his medical profession so ardently. "I guess even doctors can become ill once in awhile," he continued just as his hand landed on the small vial.

"Is a poultice needed, dear?" Anna inquired.

"No, I will be fine, dear," John responded. He took a large glass vessel filled with water and placed two drops of the golden liquid from the vial into it, watching them slowly float to the bottom. John stirred the water, which made a yellowish swirl, and poured a small amount of it into a drinking glass. Saluting his wife with the glass, he sipped the mixture.

"Oh, good, you are both home," Carrie said as she walked into the sitting room parlor. "I have something to tell you."

"Yes, what is your news, Carrie?" Anna asked.

"Well, as you know, for the past several years I have been writing Aunt Clara instructing her to share my words with William. Well, I have decided to visit him and ask if he wants to return to San Francisco to live with me," Carrie took a long deep breath, and then looked up to meet her parents' eyes.

"Oh, Carrie, my dear, are you sure this would be best? I mean, after all, he is just a young boy. How can he make that decision? And what of Clara and Walter? How will they take this news?" Anna asked, and she drifted down upon the nearest fainting sofa.

"Your mother is right, Carrie. Young William is in no position to make a decision such as this. Visiting him is one thing, but returning with him, well, that just is not the best plan, as I see it," Carrie's father offered. "Also, how could you bring him to live with you in your little upstairs apartment? There is no room to raise a young child."

"But my heart aches to have him near me, Father. I must go by train to visit my son," Carrie announced.

"Yes, I will arrange a trip for you to travel to your aunt's house to visit William. Just remember, no talk of his coming back with you to Clara; her heart would be broken. You can understand that, can you not?" Carrie's father stood near and offered his daughter a hug.

"I understand, Father, but my heart is breaking," Carrie said flatly and turned to walk away. "Make the plans for two weeks from today. I want to leave as soon as possible."

"Yes, Carrie, I will arrange the trip for you. Do you want your mother to accompany you? I highly suggest it," John said with authority.

"No, Father," Carrie said as she left the room. "I want to do this myself."

As Carrie sat in her train car staring out the window, her eyes did not see the view of the landscapes that passed so quickly. Her thoughts were on her son, whom she had not seen in three years. She felt a pain in her chest as the image of William filled her memory and she placed her white gloved hand over her heart. There were no other passengers sitting near her, which made the trip more private, just the way she desired. Arriving at the familiar station, she spied the Muirs' buggy and marched directly to it to find her uncle ready to help her into the carriage.

"Hello, Uncle Walter, how are you and Clara?" Carrie politely inquired.

"We are both fine, Carrie, and happy to have you visit with us again," Walter offered.

"And William? Does he know I am coming to visit him?" Carrie tentatively asked.

"Oh yes, my dear. Clara made sure he knew of your arrival," Walter said as they started the short ride to the house.

When Carrie stepped out of the buggy, her foot had barely touched the ground when she heard William shout, "Carrie, Carrie… how fun to have you visit us!" William ran to be at Carrie's side.

"Oh, William, give me a big hug, my boy!" Carrie said and quickly bent down to kneel at his height, not concerned with dirtying her skirt.

William offered his little outstretched arms and she fell inside them immediately, with a release of breath she had not noticed had been restrained. *How can I leave this precious little boy ever again?* Carrie thought to herself. She cupped William's face in her hands to position him directly in front of her own to search for his reaction to her affections.

"Mama... Carrie is here; Carrie is here!" shouted William as Clara came close to them.

Carrie's heart sank to the pit of her stomach as she managed to pull herself up to lean against a piece of luggage. Had she heard her son's words correctly?

"Welcome, Carrie, dear," Clara said, giving Carrie a hug. "You must be tired and in need of nourishment. Come, we will put your things in a room upstairs where you can rest and refresh yourself in privacy."

"Thank you, Aunt Clara; I am rather tired, I believe," Carrie said and slowly walked up the stairs to a prepared room. She sank upon the bed, trying to decide whether her hearing had deceived her. Her mind kept repeating the words, Mama... Mama. She gathered her thoughts enough to splash a bit of cool water from the wash basin onto her wrists and neck, and then gazed out the window at the yard below. There were wooden toys and a little wagon in one area by the front porch. She removed the hair pin from her hat and placed it and the hat on the oak dresser. *What am I thinking?* Carrie thought. *How am I to be a mother to William, when clearly, he already has one?*

Carrie enjoyed her visit with her relatives, and especially William, who had grown into such a handsome little boy. As the days passed during Carrie's stay, it became more obvious to her that to remove William from the family he had known would be unjust. She did tell him, however, that she hoped he would get to ride the train one day to visit where she lived. Carrie also told him she would continue to mail him picture cards and letters, hoping he would soon write his own letters to send back to her. William agreed and offered another big hug to his aunt Carrie.

William did visit his aunt Carrie just after his tenth birthday. He begged his mother and father to take him to the great city of San Francisco, and they all rode the train to stay with Carrie's parents. The visit was pleasant but retained an air of stress for John and Anna, who needed to control their natural instincts to reveal to William the connection between them. They had promised Clara and Walter they would not tell William the true situation, but allow Carrie or Clara to tell him when they felt it appropriate. Carrie also kept the promise during their stay and remained William's Aunt Carrie for the entire visit.

Carrie was able to take William to see the Cliff House and walk the shoreline that she had described to him in her letter a few years earlier. William was thrilled with the city of San Francisco and delighted in riding the trolley cars and listening to the sea birds over his head. When it was time for the Muirs to leave, Carrie assured William she would come to visit him soon. He gave her a big hug and told her that one day he would come back to San Francisco to study at the university.

The next two years passed quickly. Carrie and William's letters continued, and he was eager to have Carrie's suggestions as to the newest books to read that would further his education. Just before William's twelfth birthday on March 17th, he received this letter from his Aunt Carrie:

> My dear William,
>
> I am writing this letter to reach you before your birthday because Aunt Clara and I agreed when you became a young man, I was to share with you a truth you do not yet realize. As you read my words, William, try to feel them in your soul for your mind will rebel. First and foremost, you know I love you dearly and that I desire in no way to hurt your senses. Second, when you have completed reading my letter, go to Clara; she can hold you tight and tell you more of this letter's revealing truth.
>
> William, it is with love in my heart and pride in whom you have become, that I reveal to you: You are my son.
>
> The facts to this truth have been hidden for "my" benefit because of societal mores, as I was not married when you were born. You have done nothing to warrant a modicum of displeasure from me or your grandparents, John and Anna. Your loving adoptive mother and father, Clara and Walter, have been angels in your life, and mine as well.
>
> Now, my dear William, go to your mother, Clara, and place your confusion upon her breast, for she will

listen and hold you tight until you have fulfilled your
questions. I will always love you.

Your Mother,
Carrie

William reread the letter many times to grasp each word. He
realized deep inside that he had always known the truth that Carrie
shared in her letter. Several times, he found himself looking into a
mirrored glass to study the face that resembled his aunt's so clearly.
Telling this to Clara, William allowed her words to fill his mind and he
felt only joy at learning the woman whom he had called Aunt Carrie
was, in fact, his own mother. He quickly sat to write her a letter to
relinquish any fears Carrie might keep in revealing her relationship to
him. He also told his mother, Clara, how much he loved her and
Walter for their love and direction.

Carrie went to bed early the night of April 17, 1906. Her long hair
floated to the soft pillow as she lay upon her bed. Her day had
consisted of walking many blocks to check on her patients' needs, and
then riding the trolley across the city. She went to visit her parents to
inform them she had revealed to William that they were his
grandparents. Anna and John were both delighted that they could now
envelope William with the love they had stored within their hearts for
the past twelve years.

"Can I write young William as his grandmother, Carrie?" Anna
asked of her daughter.

"Yes, Mother. He is now a young man and can understand your
need to free your emotions. I have asked Aunt Clara if they can bring
William to visit with us again soon to talk in person of his rightful
heritage," Carrie explained to her mother and father.

"Yes, it is good that he know of us and how we can be of help to
his life as a Williamson," John suggested.

"Father, it will be only William's decision if he will accept his
heritage or the name of Williamson. He has known himself as a Muir
for twelve years and may not wish to change his position. Be aware of
your words, Father; let William direct you," Carrie strongly interjected.

"Yes, my dear. I agree with you," Carrie's mother offered as she
glanced at her husband. "We can only be here to love young William
and support his chosen life."

"Thank you, Mother," Carrie said and hugged her mother briefly. "So, Father, do you also agree?"

"Yes. I see that your influence is best in this case," John agreed.

"I expect William and the Muirs to arrive within a few months' time. Perhaps, one day, William will even agree to stay for an extended visit!" Carrie exclaimed, her eyes glowing with excitement.

That night, as Carrie's eyes closed to receive the dreams she knew were waiting for her, she spoke softly to the night air, "Be sure, dear William, we will be together one day."

Carrie was awakened very early the following morning to the loud sounds of the entire building violently shaking! She sat upright, frozen to the sound of cracking and rumbling. She felt as if her body would be thrown from her bed! As the noise became louder, she shouted out with unbelievable fear. She gathered her bed covers around her, thinking this must be an earthquake and that she should stay as still as she could until it was over. The wild shaking of the room targeted the pictures on the walls as they fell to the floor. She could hear the china pieces from within the cabinet in the dining room break as they also plummeted to the floor.

Carrie's body was still frozen as the shaking subsided and all she heard were the sirens of the fire wagons and the tearful screams from the streets below. After a few more minutes, she managed to move her legs and stood like a limp doll holding the bedpost for support. She slowly hobbled toward the broken window to witness the yellow flames shooting upward, surrounding her building.

Carrie's thoughts went to her patients and how she must throw on a covering to go check on them. She grabbed a long black cape, quickly putting it around her shoulders, and a hair pin to wind her hair in a knot at the back of her head. Her body was shaking as she took a deep breath. She opened the loft door and started down the long narrow stairwell. Within a few steps, Carrie was met by thick black smoke and the burning heat from the fire below. She grasped the handrail and ran back up the stairs to her loft, closed the door, and went to the window. She screamed and screamed, "Help, help... someone help me! I am up here!"

The streets were filled with smoke and there was chaos throughout the city. Carrie's shouts went unheeded as she covered her mouth with a cloth, trying to catch her breath. The smoke was seeping into her loft and she knew the effects it would take if she could not be freed soon.

She lay back down upon her bed and whispered, "My dear, William, I am so sorry. I love you."

Carrie was rescued later that day as the fires surrounding her building were contained. She was unconscious and taken to the Park Emergency Hospital. The next day, on April 19th, Carrie Williamson succumbed to smoke inhalation and minor burns without regaining consciousness. Her name was among those listed in the *San Francisco Chronicle* under the hospital's notification of patients who had been admitted on that day after the devastating earthquake shook the city on April 18, 1906.

The news of the great San Francisco earthquake traveled quickly, and when Clara and Walter told William of the death of his mother, he was stricken with grief beyond measure. As soon as the trains were running again, the Muirs took William to visit his grandparents and witness the ruins of the once beautiful city. The Williamsons' home was not destroyed, but the entire city was filled with debris. It took great tact for John to hold young William back from crossing through the shambles to locate the apartment building where his mother had lived. They had buried Carrie's body in a family plot that they took William to visit. He was consumed with grief.

William returned to live with the Muirs until he completed his early studies. His desire was to attend the university in San Francisco as he had declared he would to Carrie. When he was eighteen years old, he and the Muirs moved to a restored San Francisco so he could be near the area where his mother had lived and died. William was unable to continue his university studies as his health became poor. By the time he turned twenty-three years old, in March of 1916, he was barely able to walk. On November 4, 1916, William died of a broken heart.

Burning of San Francisco after 1906 Earthquake (Arnold Genthe)

Eleven

Infinitely large and infinitely small;
no difference, for definitions have vanished
and no boundaries are seen.
So too with Being and non-Being.

Chien-chih Seng-ts'an
Zen Patriarch, 606 AD

Moving to Hidden Valley Lake in northern California was one of the best decisions David and I had ever made. The slower paced country living fit us perfectly in our retirement years and it continues to do so for me today. The air here is pure, the land is rich, and the animal and bird life can keep me busy for hours. There are hundreds of deer that roam the neighborhood; they softly tiptoe between properties, rightly assuming they are the primary residents and they can go anywhere they please. The community supports this behavior by stopping for families of deer crossing the streets any time of day or night. Not as common to spy are the wild turkeys! They strut up and down the hills, trying to impress everyone with their regal posture and loud squawking. There are gray squirrels, jack rabbits the size of small dogs, coyotes, and a few bobcats, which are usually only seen at night. David and I loved to feed all the birds just to keep them coming back so we could to listen to their songs.

Technically, we were both retired after our move. David could not sit still, however, and became a volunteer for the Habitat for Humanity organization. He helped build many of the homes for local qualifying families. He also volunteered his many talents to those in need through his church. I also needed more to my days than designing and making my handmade jewelry, so I worked on-call for a local recovery center. I had the opportunity to complete another manuscript for a dear friend who had passed away, and I was able to get it published. David's and my relationship had become the loving marriage we had dreamed it would be when he first watched me practice cheerleading on the front lawn.

David and I felt blessed to live so close to Cindy and her family and they drove up regularly to visit and stay with us to enjoy the lakes and surrounding area. We all went on camping trips and watched our grandson grow into a handsome young man over the years. Admittedly, when our son, Rich, moved to be closer to us all, our lives were filled with turmoil once again. David and I struggled to stay on the same track with our reactions to Rich's roller coaster life with alcoholism. When Rich passed away, we learned to stay strong in our spiritual beliefs and in our love for each other. It was during this time in our lives, with the many questions darting through our minds about why Rich had died so young, that we made our pact that whichever one of us passed first to the other side, he or she would connect in some fashion with the one left behind. We wanted to share with the one remaining whatever information we could about the afterlife that we believed existed and any factual information about our belief in reincarnation.

I finished reading the details from Tablet #10 of David's and my lifetime together as mother and son. It then became very clear to me how important it was that we met in this life, had children, and lived into our later years. As I set the tablet down on the night table, I realized there were only a few tablets left to reread. I did not want to end the close connection I was feeling with David, so I reached for the next tablet.

"Iset, you look so beautiful!" Nuni exclaimed to her daughter. "Your father will be so pleased this day."

"I am so excited and a bit afraid," Iset replied.

"My dear child, why are you fearful?" Nuni asked as she combed her daughter's long hair to make it shine.

"I am not sure. Am I really old enough to be a princess? I do not feel any different than I did yesterday, Mother," Iset confided.

"You, dear Iset, are your father's daughter, first in line to become a Nubian Queen! Do not doubt your capabilities, Iset. You have been raised to be held in the highest regard by our people, you *are* ready to accept this honor today that your father will bestow upon you," Nuni

The God Amun-Ra

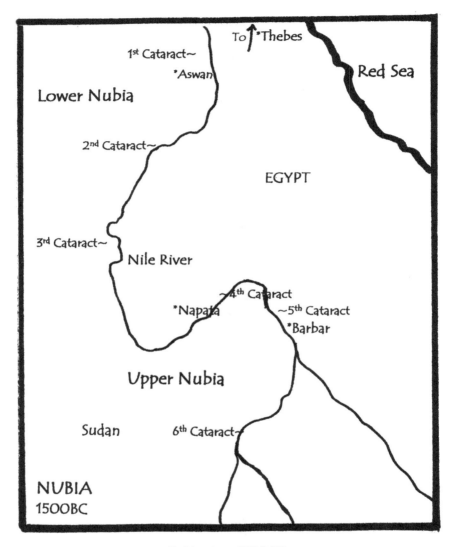

1st Cataract~
*Aswan

Lower Nubia

2nd Cataract~

EGYPT

Red Sea

To ↑ *Thebes

3rd Cataract~

Nile River

~4th Cataract
*Napata   ~5th Cataract
                 *Barbar

Upper Nubia

Sudan   6th Cataract~

NUBIA
1500BC

Nubia circa 1500 BC

said, looking Iset straight in the eyes to add emphasis to her words.

"Yes, Mother... I will accept my destiny with pride. I will be honored as the new princess of our tribe," Iset said, trying to sound more certain in the new role to be given her in the upcoming ceremonial procession.

"Are you ready?" Iset's younger sister asked. Her eyes widened as she stared at Iset. "You are truly a princess, my sister!"

Iset was draped with gold-lined cloth, which ended at her feet. Her headdress sparkled with jewels set into a golden crown. There were silver rings hanging from her ears and gold bracelets around her upper arms. Placed on all of Iset's fingers were gold and silver rings with large jewels matching her crown. Nuni painted Iset's lips deep red and lined her eyes black to resemble Egyptian royalty.

"Yes, go tell your father we will be seen by our people soon," Nuni spoke in reply. Turning to Iset, Nuni said, "Dear daughter, you are ready. Your people are ready and waiting. Blessed are we." Nuni took Iset's hands in her own, closed her eyes, and recited a prayer to the god Amun-Ra for Iset's protection.

Nuni and Iset greeted Chief Kabin on that early morning of the ceremonial procession as people gazed upon their new princess of Barbar. Their tribe was not large, but they commanded respect and earned it among the other Nubian tribes. Chief Kabin ruled over those who were farmers and cattlemen. The steer were plentiful in the Upper Nubian Desert near the 5th Cataract, and they were an easy offering to the Egyptians. The Barbar would travel from the Nile River to the inner Sudan, tending their cattle and farming lands without fear of being ravaged by the Egyptian soldiers. They were established as a colony to produce their goods for King Thutmose II, reigning Pharaoh of Egypt.

Chief Kabin and Nuni inherited their high status after the tribe migrated from the West, beyond the Red Sea in the East. Kabin allowed many of the nomads along the way to travel with their party as they transported large herds of cattle. The steer were revered by the people, and it was an honor to be of service on this route. When the Egyptians traveled south into the Upper Nubian region, they followed the Nile. The Barbar would gather their offerings and meet the soldiers on the banks of the great river to make their trade. It was Kabin who made friends with the soldiers and assured them his tribe would continue to bring more cattle for the pharaoh. The tribe would make this trip twice each year, all orchestrated by Kabin. The Barbar tribe grew annually with each journey. Soon, the tribe pronounced him Chief Kabin. Today, Kabin's daughter, Iset, would be named high princess and would one day rule the tribe as its queen.

As the Egyptian culture became more infused into the Lower and Upper Cataracts of Nubia, their spiritual beliefs also reached the tribal people. Nuni felt strongly about the goddess, Isis, and named her daughter, Iset, which meant Isis in the Nubian language. Iset was a beautiful young woman with long silken black hair and eyes lighter than most Nubians. Her long legs were sleek and strong and she carried her body with a regal air. At fifteen years old, Iset was surely a royal beauty. She was carried high over the heads of the tribe's people during the ceremony, on an open litter decorated with red and yellow flowers streaming down its sides. More flowers and vials of essence were tossed at her side as she passed the crowds. Iset waved her hand and began to feel like a princess after all.

"Chief Kabin! Chief Kabin! The Egyptian soldiers are coming early and they are riding fast," shouted a tribesman running through the crowds.

"Make haste; pass this news to the herdsmen to have our offering ready!" Kabin shouted back to him.

The ceremony for Iset was ending and soon the entire colony was rushing around to make ready for the arrival of the pharaoh's soldiers. Mothers tucked their children safely out-of-sight and told their young daughters to run to the far end of the trees along the waters of the Nile. Iset remained in her ceremonial attire, thinking she should now stand beside her father and mother as high princess.

Besides their cattle, the people of Barbar had palettes of quartz, ostrich feathers, and copper weapons to offer the pharaoh. Tribesmen and women dashed to gather their bounty to put before the feet of the soldiers. The soldiers arrived, swirling the dust of the desert with them. There were dozens of soldiers and four horse drawn chariots. First and foremost, the riders were fed and given all the wine they desired. Soon, a procession of steer, jewelry made from gold and silver, leather goods, and other items of trade would be set before the emissaries. Many times, if an item was not seen but was desired, a soldier would threaten to slash off the head of the closest man, woman, or steer until the treasure was brought before him. Fearing that one of their tribesmen might be sacrificed, Kabin ordered all goods to be readily accessible. Wisely, he knew the soldiers could not travel far if they chose to take

King Thutmose II

everything, so he held back nothing except their food supply and the hidden children.

The head soldier of the Egyptian army was a familiar face to Kabin; they had completed trades many times. Kabin felt him to be a fair man. "I lay before the great soldier of our pharaoh all the bounty of our land for your choosing," Chief Kabin announced as he bowed from his waist.

"Good day to you, Kabin, and how is your colony this fine day?" the soldier replied.

"We are in good spirits, sir. I assume your ride was pleasant?" Kabin asked, handing the soldier a vessel of wine.

"We have ridden long and hard this trip. Our king, Thutmose II, is seeking much for his kingdom. We have made several visits along the Nile to obtain our goods; your colony is our last stop. Our chariots are filled, but we wish to take some of your finest cattle this day," the soldier said with a commanding tone.

"Yes, yes. Indeed, sir, we have several of the finest cattle in the Cataract. Let us show you the parade," Kabin said and waved his arm toward the herdsmen to bring the steer.

As the cattle passed before them, the head soldier nodded with approval at the animals to be taken. When this procession was complete, Kabin suggested the trader look at the finery of gold jewelry recently made. He waved his arm toward the goldsmiths to bring their goods to display.

While the soldier was deciding upon which pieces to place in his leather bag, he slowly glanced upward, catching the beauty of Iset. "My, my, what do we have here?" he said loudly with his crooked smile showing yellowing teeth.

"May I present, Iset, my daughter and princess to the people of Barbar," Kabin responded.

"Where have you been hiding this pretty thing, Kabin?" asked the soldier without acknowledging the introduction. "Our pharaoh needs a few new slaves. Do you have more like this one?"

"We have agreed that if our colony produces the cattle you desire, you will not take our women and children from us!" Kabin said firmly.

"Oh, but that agreement was made purely between yourself and me, without our king's knowledge. Now we are instructed to bring him new slaves, women and men!" the soldier spouted.

"Dear sir, I cannot fight you and your army. But please do not take my own daughter!" Kabin begged the soldier.

"It is done!" the soldier shouted. He dismounted his steed and grabbed Iset by the arm, dragging her toward the closest chariot. There were four girls and two young women standing shoulder to shoulder in the chariot; they squeezed together even more to make room for Iset.

"Father, Father... please do not let them take me!" Iset screamed, but her screams went unheeded. Iset turned to look back at her mother and father as the chariot left swiftly with the dust from the galloping horses.

Iset never saw her mother and father again. Chief Kabin outlived his wife, Nuni, by five years. After his daughter was taken from him, his reign over the Barbar colony became one he no longer desired. He chose to take his family, and any tribesmen who wished to follow, to the Eastern deserts of the Red Sea once again. Kabin returned to the land of his father, not wishing to be subjected any longer to the cruel Egyptian kingdom.

ॐ

Why must life on Earth be so difficult? I thought as I laid down the tablet. I remembered reading something that David had relayed to me while I was channeling his words, and I went to find the binder of notes. In one passage, in response to my question about violence, David said: *We incarnate upon the planet Earth to experience all experiences.* A revelation to be sure! This explains why so much of our lives is consumed with suffering, pain, loss, violence, and the emotions of anger, fear, jealousy, and deceit. If our souls' lifetimes must experience all there is to be experienced on Earth, and on other planes, it must be how our souls' evolutionary journey strives ultimately to meet and join with the Divine Power, or God.

I believe one of the greatest gifts we can realize while on Earth is to enjoy each day. When we allow ourselves to hear and see the world around us, a healthy perspective for life can be visualized. During the 1990s, I had the honor to be in the company of His Holiness the Dalai Lama. He spoke a few sentences which, at the time, I felt were personally directed to me. I quickly wrote them down on a small notepad:

> "Let go of all desires... it will unfold as is. It has already happened—now rewards are here for you. Rejoice—you are dancing in the sun. Look around and see your happiness. No need to want—you are here. Enjoy!"

David and Barbara in Redwoods

David and I did enjoy our life together. One of our favorite trips was taken only a few years before his death. We took the long drive on Highway 101 to venture up the California coastline to Oregon.

We wanted to experience the famous Redwood trees that line the landscape along the northern part of the state. We took our time so we could go off the highway to explore the small towns, wade in the rivers, and hike through the forests. The Redwoods have stood for thousands of years as majestic sentinels guarding the entrance to northern California from the Pacific Ocean. The smell of fresh air filled our lungs as we stopped to view the ocean where the road seemed to veer toward the edge of the world. Joseph Campbell's words rang in my ears during that journey—*Follow your bliss!*

Now, Tablet #12 was staring at me. My eyes were dry and my body needed rest, but I was drawn to read again about my life as Iset.

Iset's journey with the Egyptian soldiers was a perilous one. As the caravan of precarious chariots and lecherous soldiers made their way up the Nile, Iset felt she would surely die. When they reached the gold mines of Napata of the 4th Cataract, Iset was able to view the magnificent gold jewelry, chalices, vessels, and ornaments made by the artisans. The long journey continued to Aswan of the 1st Cataract, known for its bracelets of quartz, spices, baskets, and pottery with patterns of etched animals. Once the army and its cargo arrived at the kingdom of Thebes, Iset was taken to the baths. There she was allowed to bathe and make herself presentable. Several dozen young Nubian girls and women were there who had all been taken from their villages. Fear rose in each one as they talked of the possibilities their lives might now take. It was rumored from one to the other that the royalty of Egypt resembled animals and they ate their Nubian slaves!

Iset took extra care in applying the essence and unguents she found in the many gold and ivory flasks. She combed her ebony hair to renew its shine. She reapplied the black galena made from lead and carbon powder to her eyes, taking care to resemble the lines of the Egyptians she had seen during her journey. Finally, Iset painted her lips with the red ochre mixture found in small ivory bowls. She had transformed herself to reflect, once again, the proud princess of Barbar.

The group of Nubian women were escorted through the temple columns and told to sit on the pillows laid on the stone floor. Iset selected a position behind most of the women, thinking she would not be noticed. Her eyes widened as one guard passed by, dropping a red rose in her lap. He said no words as he continued on his way to the entrance at the far end of the hallway. Suddenly, lutes and horns filled the quarters with their music and the Egyptian pharaoh appeared. King Thutmose II was a rather short man, but most handsomely dressed in fine linens lined with gold and silver cloth. As was the custom, his face was painted with blush hues and his eyes were etched with black. He sat on a chair of ivory adorned with various precious gems. Earlier that day, the soldiers had laid their cargo from the journey upon the stairs to the royal chair in hopes their king would be pleased.

"I see your journey into the desert has fared us well! Let us celebrate our bountiful offerings from our Nubian brothers!" shouted Thutmose as he raised his silver wine chalice in a salute.

"Where shall we dispense of the Nubian slaves, my king?" asked the head soldier.

"Bring them before me to display their beauty," Thutmose commanded.

As the Nubian women were gathered in a line to parade before their king, Iset bent her head down. "Look up, child!" shouted a guard. "You are before King Thutmose II, Pharaoh of Egypt!"

Iset slowly raised her face to gaze upon the king, allowing their eyes to meet. She stood fast to assure her status of princess was recognized.

"What is your name, girl?" inquired Thutmose.

"Iset, your majesty," Iset said softly.

"Iset, that is a strange name for a Nubian girl. What does it mean?" Thutmose asked his interpreter.

"In Nubian language, it translates to our goddess, Isis, my king," he replied.

"Yes. Isis. You will be called Isis from this moment forward. Take her to my chambers," Thutmose commanded.

"And what of the others, my king?" asked the guard, Gombat.

"They will be allotted as slaves," Thutmose ordered.

Twelve

The Great Way is not difficult
for those who have no preferences.
When love and hate are both absent
everything becomes clear and undisguised.

Chien-chih Seng-ts'an
Zen Patriarch, 606 AD

Iset found herself surrounded by silk pillows, flowing scented cloth of all colors, and vessels of wine and beer. She drank the wine and tried to comprehend what was happening, and then an inner voice came to her in soft waves of visions... *You will be Isis, queen to the Pharaoh.... No need to resist; you will be honored and rewarded.* The women slaves draped her body in gold cloth. Her hair was bound high and a headdress was placed upon her head. Her face was painted with unguents and creams she had never seen before. The women asked whether she had been bedded; Iset replied she had not. They instructed her as to what to expect from their king since most of them had previously visited his bed. Iset understood the task before her.

"Isis? Your pharaoh is approaching," the handsome guard, Gombat, said as he entered the king's chamber. "Are you ready to receive him?"

"What is your name? Are you not the one who gave me the red rose?" Iset asked the guard.

"My name is Gombat. I was a slave; now I am high guard to Thutmose II, our Pharaoh of Egypt. Yes, I dropped the rose in your lap, Isis. I favored you the moment my eyes beheld your beauty," Gombat replied as he bowed to Iset.

"I favor you also, Gombat, but we must not tell of it for I am to be

The Goddess Isis

Queen Hatshepsut

bedded by Thutmose this night. What will become of me?" Iset asked the strong guard, signaling him to approach her side.

"I fear you will become a favored concubine, Isis, which breaks my heart," Gombat said with his head lowered as he bent down on one knee.

"You call me, Isis; will this be my name then?" Iset asked.

"Yes. The king has made it so. He is near and I must go this night, but I will meet you soon, my rose," Gombat promised, and then he went to stand at attention near the chamber's entrance.

Soon, Thutmose arrived in his splendor of robes and bejeweled strands of fabric draped from his neck. His stature was small and his face had been painted heavily; Iset found him to be odd-looking at best.

"Isis, your beauty glows as the sun! Come, lie near me. We will learn of each other this night." Thutmose motioned for Iset to join him on the royal bed. "Yes, my king. I owe you my life and it is yours this night." Iset laid her scented body next to Thutmose, but not too close. "I honor my new name as Isis, to reflect your goddess. My mother follows your god, Amun-Ra and his queen, my king," she offered to Thutmose.

"You are fast with words, Isis! This pleases me. My other consorts do not offer their words. You will be good company, Isis!" Thutmose said, as he put his arms around Isis, drawing her closer. The two talked for a few hours, and then Thutmose ordered all the guards and slaves to leave. He was gentle with his new virgin slave.

Isis reveled in the high status she assumed among the king's harem. She was considered the highest consort. True, Thutmose was married to his half-sister, Hatshepsut, but Isis knew only she could please her king satisfactorily. Isis was given her own chambers to secure privacy for when she entertained Thutmose. Albeit, Isis also chose to favor Gombat with her charms.

"Oh my lover, shall we never be able to bind our love?" Isis asked as she fondled Gombat's chest. "My heart aches for you each day, even when I am in the company of Thutmose. What is to become of our love, dear Gombat?"

"Isis, my rose, you are the center of my life. I cherish each moment we have together. We are meant to be together. As long as we are discreet, our love can flourish. But I fear it will never be official, for it has been rumored that Thutmose has plans for you," Gombat shared with his lover.

"Of what plans are you speaking, my lover?" Isis inquired and sat upright as if she could hear the news better sitting than reclining.

"It is said that you are to become his secondary wife, dear Isis. You would be his queen!" Gombat said, beginning to weep like a boy.

"I learned this the day I arrived in Thebes... the words came to me in a vision. Now you say they will be true?" Isis responded, knowing her question's answer.

"I fear we will never be together again, Isis... please say it will not be so," Gombat begged as he pulled his lover close to his bare chest.

"If I am to be queen, I can take lovers as I wish, dear Gombat. I will not forsake our love," Isis whispered and deeply kissed her lover to cement the oath.

Isis had been treated like royalty among the Nubian guards and slaves, and she began to enjoy the honors bestowed upon her. It was common for a pharaoh to have many slave concubines, as well as several wives, if he desired. The temples were filled with a pleasure-seeking population of royalty with casual affairs in all combinations of sexual partners. Isis learned most information from her own Nubian women attendants. They would group together at the baths to share avidly the latest rumors surrounding their wealthy masters.

The land was rich in farming and Isis was brought every kind of food imaginable. The fruit of the various melons were her favorites; however, to her delight, she was introduced to many other gluttonous pleasures. She had never tasted the meat of fowl and requested the delicacy of a duck feast to be served often. She would watch the water clock, making sure she was ready each evening when her king entered her chambers. If he did not arrive, Isis would send for Gombat to share her bed. When she became ill from overeating, her guard would summon the royal healers to offer her potions of herbs and salts to ingest for their laxative effects. Isis became curious as to the healer's methods and requested a lesson.

"What are your remedies for the wounds of our soldiers?" Isis asked one healer who was tending her.

"I use the bee honey in the copper jars to soothe the wound, and then I apply willow bark to help it heal," replied the healer.

"And what of women's pains?" Isis inquired.

"Are you in pain, Isis?" he asked.

"No, I am curious about the healings you perform. What do you use for women's pain, down here?" Isis asked again, holding her lower abdomen.

"There is much mystery to a woman's body, Isis. I would suggest wearing an amulet around the neck filled with fennel seed and herbs of mint," the healer revealed. "If you need such an amulet, I will make it for you."

"No, no, I am fine at present. Tell my guards and women they may return to my chambers now," Isis instructed.

The guards stood fast at the chambers' entrance and the Nubian slaves returned. "Let us play a game of senet!" Isis exclaimed. "Where are the sticks?"

Just as the game started, a surprise visit from Thutmose was announced by the guard. "Isis... I have come to tell you of a revelation!" he shouted as he bounced into the room.

"What is it, my king?" Isis asked, thinking she already knew his secret.

"You will become my wife, Isis!" said the king with his arms opening wide for his lover to enter.

"Oh, my king, can such magic transpire?" Isis shyly asked.

"I will make it so, dear Isis. You have been my confidant and lover; now you will be my wife. As I told you, Hatshepsut was taken as a wife for reasons of politics, but you, Isis, will be my royal secondary wife. My heart is beating so fast I think it shall burst!" Thutmose said, and he held Isis close to his chest.

"When will the ceremony take place, my king?" Isis inquired.

"On the moon's fullness next. Be ready, dear lover; we will share my seat of royalty together and for always. You will give me the son Hatshepsut has not, to ensure my succession!" He twirled around in pleasure falling with dizziness onto the pillows that had received his body so many times before. Isis joined her royal lover and king to talk more of the wedding plans.

Early the next morning after Thutmose had left her bed, Isis summoned Gombat to join her in her chambers. "Oh my dear, Gombat! Your prediction has come to pass!" Isis cried out.

"I have been informed, my rose. Have you accepted the proposal?" Gombat asked between his tears.

"How could I not? He is our king," Isis said as she touched his tears with her fingers and placed them on her lips. "Remember, dear lover, we can always be together. Soon, I will be your queen and will have authority to choose my lovers as I please," Isis said reassuringly.

"But what if the king is informed of our meetings, Isis? I fear he will ban me from the temples, or cut off my head!" Gombat said, lowering his voice so as not to alarm the guards and slaves. "Please tell me again we will always be together, dear Isis."

"Yes, always, Gombat... always and forever," Isis whispered in his ear.

❧

Isis was lavished with oils for her hair and flower scents bathed her body. She ordered the women to leave her head free from any headdress for she knew a queen's crown would be placed upon it soon. Her robes were golden silk from the lands beyond those of the north regents, and arm bracelets set with jewels adorned both arms. She was told by one of the old women to leave her breast covered only in cloth, leaving necklaces behind. "You would not want to be too bold in appearance as a secondary wife," the woman advised.

"You have given me good advice, old woman, reminding me of my dear mother, Nuni. I only hope she and Father will know of my chosen life," Isis said and sighed a long breath, then continued, "When I am with child for our pharaoh, will you be first to tend me?"

"If you wish, Isis, I will guide your labors," replied the old attendant. "Now, it is time for your entrance into the public chambers of our pharaoh to become his queen!"

Pyramids in Nubia

Queen Isis

Isis walked through the masses of people who gathered to glance upon the new chosen wife of their king. Her steps were long and straight; her head held high in confidence to accept her destiny. She stood before her king a good six inches taller, but Isis kept her stance, knowing Thutmose loved her long legs and would not wish her to appear anything less than she was. The ceremony ended with Isis receiving a jeweled headdress made to fit her, and the couple walked the grounds to greet their guests. The halls and chambers were filled with the sounds of flute and harp while the guests danced and laughed through the night.

Isis knew she had been destined to be royalty to her own tribe from Barbar; however, she accepted her new position as queen to her pharaoh with pride and honor. She was escorted in a covered litter on journeys with Thutmose and his soldiers to admire the lands under their rule. Isis was amazed to view the many obelisks and pyramids holding the remains of Egypt's past royalty. She delighted in the many farming and cattle territories that reminded her of her tribal family. Their travels took them all the way to the 4th Cataract and Napata to see the gold mines, but they did not go beyond that point along the Nile. Isis was told the caravan would not visit Barbar. Upon her request, Thutmose sent soldiers to inform her family of their marriage.

It was not long after this long journey that Isis became pregnant. She gave birth to a healthy son and presented him to Thutmose. "My king, I give to you this son to be your heir."

"He shall be named Thutmose III and become my successor!" announced Thutmose. "Isis, you will tend to his every need and see to it while I am away on campaign that he grows in fine stature. He must learn to use the bow expertly and to sit a horse as royalty. See to it that Hatshepsut does not influence him with her idle pleasures. Thutmose must become the next ruler of Egypt and know the languages of our regions. He must command his people with gentle force. All these things you must accomplish for my son, Isis; do you understand?"

"Yes, dear husband. I will see to it myself," Isis replied.

For two years, King Thutmose campaigned to add more territory to the east and south regions. He ordered his men to fight hard for their kingdom. His health became questionable due to the stressful methods he employed to take possession of more and more land and its bounty. Soon, Thutmose fell ill. Isis summoned all the healers in the lands to tend to her husband. Each tried a different method to rid their king of his disease. In the end, Thutmose succumbed. Isis became overruled by

Hatshepsut's power as first wife and Queen of Egypt. Hatshepsut ordered the body of her husband to be mummified and buried in a pyramid tomb.

"Hatshepsut, I do not know you well, but it was our husband's wish that his son, Thutmose III, become Pharaoh of Egypt at his demise. Will you allow this wish, or do I need to summon the official regents to enforce it?" Isis asked with sternness in her voice.

"I will see to it. Your life here is done. I will reign as co-regent with young Thutmose until he has completed his training and makes his choice of how to rule. You, Isis, are to be left in our departed husband's tomb to die beside your king!" Hatshepsut ordered and waved her hand for the guards to take her away.

Isis was compliant with her destiny, for this was an accepted burial ritual among Egyptian royalty. To die beside one's king was considered a privilege and Isis knew this was to be her fate. She went to speak to her son one last time. He was a mere two years old, and even though he did not understand her words, he nodded his head in agreement that he must do what his stepmother ordered. Then Isis asked her guard to summon Gombat to her chambers.

"My lover for all times, I must leave you today for my place is in eternity with our king," Isis said with tears running down her cheeks.

"No, Isis. You will not be alone. I will go with you, my rose, for our love must never end," Gombat said as he held Isis close.

Hatshepsut's guards entered the chamber. They broke the lovers' embrace and took Isis away.

"My friends," Gombat shouted to the guards, "wait! Take me also!"

The pair was left inside the Pharaoh's tomb with much of his wealth and treasures to survive through eternity where they would meet again in the afterlife. There were several other loyal slaves and concubines who accompanied Isis and Gombat into the tomb, and then the granite stones were closed behind them forever.

The son of Isis, Thutmose III, grew to be a wise and honored ruler of Egypt for fifty-four years. He was an avid sportsman who led hunts for lion and elephant. The son of Isis also became a great builder of temples and pyramids. Like his father before him, he accompanied his army campaigns to conquer extended regions to his rule. His wisdom in policy was highly recognized when he ordered the princes of conquered regions to go to Thebes where they were educated in the ways of cooperation instead of rebellion. They were then allowed to return to their homeland to instruct this harmonious behavior to their people. Thutmose III became a model for later Egyptians; he was remembered by this hymn, in which Amun-Ra proclaimed:

I set thy glory and the fear of thee in all lands,
and the terror of thee as far as the four supports of the sky.
The rulers of all foreign countries are gathered together within thy grasp.
I stretch out my hands to bind them for thee.

King Thutmose III

Thirteen

*We should not hold rigidly to our personal views
but enter into dialogue in an open-minded way.
In this way we will be able to compare
viewpoints and discover new ones.*

His Holiness The Dalai Lama
Daily Advice from the Heart

I searched for the box of tissue on the night table to blow my nose and wipe the tears from my face. Laying the last tablet down beside me, I whispered to David, "Thank you for keeping our pact, honey. I will always cherish these lifetimes you have shared with me. My soul honors your soul, and I know we will be together again to experience even more lifetime lessons. When the timing is right, I will share your words, your *Story of Heaven*. I will also share the stories of our lifetimes to affirm that our souls do experience many incarnations to journey through our many lessons."

It has been over two years since David passed to the other side on July 22, 2011. The following pages contain much of my personal journaling after David's sudden death, and my search for answers beyond my human knowledge. As a child, I had many psychic experiences ranging from seeing strange people and/or beings in my room at night to having several precognitive dreams. These abilities diminished in my adult years; however, many times in the 1980s, I was able to connect in deep meditation with a few of my past lifetimes. I was rewarded with more details about my adventurous soul by looking up the names and dates in the encyclopedia set I had at the time. This was before the Internet and Google Search. My research revealed the verification of my Egyptian lifetime as Isis. This information and the details of

David's channeled words completed this lifetime for me.

Throughout my adult life, I have had many questions about life after death, soul journeys, the birth of a soul, and other metaphysical topics. I studied human consciousness for most of my life, and became a psychospiritual therapist after obtaining my master's and doctoral degrees. While working with my patients to guide them toward healing, many times I used age regression techniques to discover within their childhood where their issues had originated. I used clinical hypnotherapy to guide them gently toward a pre-appointed age and audio-taped their sessions, so they could later hear and understand what had transpired. When one is in a deep state of relaxed hypnosis, what transpires is usually not remembered.

I discovered a delightful surprise with many of my patients that as they were regressing to their younger years, they would skip right into a past lifetime! These clients would relate detailed images, dates, names, and experiences as the tape recorder was spinning their tales. To me, these flashbacks into another time and space confirmed my strong inner-knowing of the reality of reincarnation.

Through the years, I shared with David the few glimpses of other lifetimes that I felt we had experienced together. He may not have totally believed it all, but he listened in respect for my strong convictions. As the fifty-year mark of our relationship approached, we made a pact that whoever passed away first would connect with the other to confirm, or not, my belief in reincarnation.

David peacefully glided from this Earth during the same week when we had met fifty years prior, in 1961. After I received the detailed information about our lifetimes together through David's channeled words, I was able to validate some of the people's lives by conducting Internet searches through websites such as Ancestry.com and the online encyclopedia, Wikipedia. Again, this was done *after* David's death, when I began channeling his words. The following few pages are from my personal journal as I was grieving David's death. Then, the following two chapters include the communication I channeled from him about heaven: "David's Story of Heaven."

Early August 2011 (Two weeks after David's passing)

Honey? Are you there? My first touch from your soul came today as I was driving over the hill to a doctor's appointment. I turned on a new Josh Groban CD and a song rang in my ears with so much emotion that I needed to pull off the road; I burst into tears and decided not to listen to it while I was driving. When I returned home, I took the CD out of the car and put it in the player in the kitchen. The song was so powerful even though I knew nothing of what Marco Marinangel's lyrics meant, for they were all in Italian!

I knew that you had sent me this song and that I must find out what the words were saying. So I got on the computer and found a translator website from Italian to English. Again, I have never done this, so I felt very guided by you even to come up with the idea. Oh, honey, the song you sent me touched me so very deeply... here are a few lines:

Farewell Time

My heart fears to leave you
A difficult moment
As if a knife tears you.
Believe me, it hurts having to go away
To know that you suffer
As I suffer, when it is
The time of farewell.
Please know that my choice
Is a sign that love never dies
Do not hate me
Keep your happiness.
It will be hard to ignore the memories of this life
Everything reminds me
That you are a part of me.

Late September 2011

The days are passing so slowly and the nights drag on until I finally get up and roam the house. I am still asking questions about why you needed to go at this time, David. Was it something physical, like too much blood pressure medication? Did your soul need to leave to be with Rich? Did you have any idea you were going to leave so young? Were you hurting physically or emotionally, but didn't tell me?

So many questions that will go unanswered: Will you come to me in a dream? Have you already done so and I don't remember? Can you make the chimes ring when there is no wind? This has happened several times. Can you direct my attention to things like the Josh Groban song?

Every time I think of you standing near me with your smile, your touch, I cry inside. To remember you hurts... hurts my heart.

Learning to live alone sucks. Learning to live without you? I am not sure I want to. It's hard to think of all the days I will have in which you will not be with me. I think being left when another dies is harder than leaving first. At least when one dies, there is closure of that life and a time to move forward. I feel no closure and cannot move forward... yet. Will there be a time when I can move on? I cannot even imagine that life.

I am putting so much hope and energy into my planned Ananda Village trip in October... will you join me there? Will the silence bring you to me?

Later September 2011

Some say I must get on with my life; others give me permission to linger in grief's limbo. I am caught between wanting to move forward and wanting to stay close to you. If I move on toward a new beginning, will I lose your essence around me? I feel you so close these days—do you feel me? Can you feel my emotions? Do you know how much I miss you, David?

The winter is coming fast... should I put things up off the porch? Should I put away the stuff on the side of the house? Should I cover the chairs and table? It seems that now there is so much for me to do, alone. I do appreciate your re-roofing the house so the rain will not enter in future years. I know you were so proud to have gotten that project almost completed. You took so much pride in your work; in fact, your work was always a priority, but not before your family. Work, not words, was your forte. Such a hard worker and such a silent bear you were.

When I allow my thoughts to go to our life together, I begin to cry—we had such a great beginning and later years together, didn't we? So in love, so fast and so young.

Writing in my journal seems to help me—if you are around me, thank you. I will need your strength to go forward. In whatever I choose to do with the rest of my life, please be beside me, dear David. Help me to know which directions are best for me to pursue, which decisions to make to keep in touch with my principles and soul purpose—you can guide me now like never before.

The deer miss you, honey. They see me, but they know it is not you bringing them bites of fruit or filling the water pan. They know you are gone. Did I tell you about the dream I had within a few weeks of your leaving? All the animals and birds in the backyard and from the hill were on the far side of the fence—just staring at me in silent mourning.

It was so beautiful—they were honoring you and trying to comfort me.

Now, every time I go outside to fill the water trough, our chimes sing their song of harmony and peace. I am telling you this, but I know you are ringing them! Because even when there is no wind whatsoever, they sound their music to me whenever I go outside. Thank you for being so near, knowing that I would know you have visited me once again.

Grief's Shadow

I am living in our physical dimension; my son and husband are living in theirs. I sense the connection—like the sound of my chimes' vibration.

I sit, I listen intently. If I were deaf, would I grieve in this manner?

My birds are balanced on the backyard fence, playing tag. The wind chimes singing their metal tune claiming the air with sound.

Fall seems imminently close—I will miss the rays of light glittering off the cottonwood leaves. I will miss the warm mornings on the deck silently listening.

My hummingbirds venture to hang in the air two feet from my face to whisper thoughts of healing.

The summer squash is nearly ready—sweet yellow jewels.

Mr. Jay picks at his black seeds, bobbing his head in thanks. Where are you now, David? In a classroom of spirits reflecting past journeys? Sitting beside me smiling that little smile? Flying again with loved ones? Where have you gone my beloved?

Our fruit trees withheld their fruit this year and David left…

End of September 2011

Hi, Honey… I had a good night's sleep last night, probably because I took a sleeping pill again. But it feels good to have a complete sleep through the night. I have been thinking about what I am learning because of your leaving. One thing for sure is that I am not as strong emotionally as I had thought. I have broken down in tears so many times, and you know I am not one to cry that often. My emotional state is unbalanced for sure. I am still hoping to get more balanced on my trip to the Ananda Village and to sit in silence.

I see people walking their dogs each morning now that the weather has cooled down. People are suggesting I get a dog too—maybe next year.

October 2011

Well, the trip to Ananda was postponed. It just didn't work out for either of us at this time. It will be better in the spring when the weather is warm and the flowers are in bloom. However, I put so much anticipation on going to sit in meditation and try to hear whispers from you....

> Seven black birds circling the hill
> Seven notes ring from the chimes
> One dove flies over the plum tree
> One heart is heavy today....

November 2011

Thanksgiving was so very difficult. The table was empty of half my family. Cindy and I cried a bit when we said the blessing... missing you terribly. I watched a television movie last night about a man and his wife who had died and how she visited him in spirit. Come to me, David—I will not be afraid; I will not turn away. I long for your smile and twinkling eyes to see my soul once again. I do not want to wait until I shed my body—I want to see you now. Can I continue my song? Can I hum when you cannot hear me? The tears I thought were dry are flowing again. Will I cry forever?

I was guided to walk the doggie-walk trail we walked regularly with our dear Goldie. I began to cry and looked up to spy a lone hawk fluttering above me. As you know, the hawk has been my totem animal for many years. Its presence signifies *vision* or *clear seeing*. As I stood in the morning sun, I followed the hawk as it landed in the old oak tree above me. I continued staring at him and spoke, "Thank you for visiting me. Were you sent by David?" The majestic bird sat proud and looked down at my words hanging in midair. His eyes were dark and warm. The moments spoke to me of *connection*. I cherish that walk and the hawk's message.

A Tribute to Fall

Fall is putting the lake to bed now
The leaves lay in a quilt weaving colors of
Yellow, red, and orange.
She calls Wind to roam the valleys and pine tops
She whispers for Sun to drop the horizon
She motions to Cloud to draw the shade,
And all too soon
Fall will close her eyes for Winter.

December 2011

I finally got myself out of the house and sold some of my handmade jewelry at the Christmas Boutique. People were nice and supportive of me being social again. The season sucks this year—I just want it over. I did get a small little tree to brighten my living room—Oh, my god, I said *my*, not *our*... that hurts inside, but I realize I am moving on without you, which I must see as positive.

December 30, 2011 (My birthday)

Thank you very much, dear sweet David for my fantastic dream/vision of you calling me on the phone for my birthday! I so needed to hear from you; I will remember this dream always. Many friends and family came to celebrate my birthday this year; it was a nice few days and helped to get my mind off of you.

January 2012

Ummmm, I made it to here—six months without you. This month is usually my go inside month, but somehow I am out and about more. On your birthday, January 9th, I hope you heard and saw me honor it with my ritual.

February 2012

Winter's Blessing

Winter came lightly this year
As if He knew I could not take the cold.
The hawks are out chasing a large black bird
Away from their nests
Screeching that familiar pitch in midair.
They fly as wingmen encircling the bird—
I feel protected.
My feet are moving a bit quicker now
As Winter assures me, Spring is on her way.
I will sit still and listen for Her song.

April 2012

Dear one… my days seem to pass without my knowing. The Jays are gathering for nests again and the squirrels are racing around stealing all the bird food. Some have even learned how to climb up the birdfeeder pole and jump over into the feeding gourd! I put Vaseline on the pole, hoping that would stop them; we'll see. Way too much rain this month; I am so ready for sunshine.

Channeling: David's Story of Heaven

June 2012

In a meditation, you came to me and said, "I am no longer material… I am ethereal." So does this mean the other side is made of ethers? Why do we call *it the other side*? The other side of what?

My recent trip to the Ananda Village in Nevada City, to be in silence and meditate, has helped me tremendously. I know you were with me, and the bits of information you imparted to me allowed me to think more seriously of trying to channel your words. When I asked for your connection, you were right there, saying—

> If you knew how easy it is to be here with you, you would not worry. I am so close, only a breath away. When you are more at peace with your life, I will guide you. I will share my journey here with you. As you begin to understand more, you will share this within your writing to heal the hearts of many.

Mid-August 2012

I feel I am ready to hear your words, David. If I start to put my thoughts together, would you be there when I ask? How do I ask? Is this something we can do, and should we? Each morning like this one, I will close my eyes in meditation to search for your energy.

> As you close your eyes, I will come to you through your thoughts. When you are ready to type, I will be there with you. I am always with you, Barbara. I live *in* you as you live *in* me. We are actually of the same family, the same *soul family*. As I share my existence here with you, you will understand. You must be patient, as I am moving at a much faster energy or vibration than you, and the thoughts and expressions I give

you must be slowed for you to grasp what I am sending to you. Be patient, Barbara... we will meet *where the horizon meets the sea*, as you once wrote in a poem I enjoyed.

Always with you,

David

I understand that you are with me now, David. If I sit at the computer and type with my eyes closed there will be lots of typos!

Your eyes will be closed but your mind and heart open. Trust me, Barbara; you will find there will be little edits. One thing I want to tell you is that because I am now in a nonphysical form, I am no longer the David you knew—I am much, much more. My speech will sound peculiar at first, but you will learn to understand me.

So, I will actually be channeling your words?

Yes. But remember all channeling goes through the channel's subconscious mind. Your knowledge and insight will also be of value in this writing. Do not be afraid to ask questions, yet know some of what I say will filter through your conscious mind as well. The words will be laced with your own subconscious and super-conscious awareness because you will be in an altered state as you type. Meditate first before each connection to clear your conscious mind.

But I do not want to hinder or change something that you would tell me into something I might believe or think. Will you correct me, or direct my typing if I choose the wrong word or thought?

Yes. I may sound different to you, Barbara; I am now beginning to join with my Soul Being. Just type what you hear in your mind when you choose to sit at your computer; close your eyes, and listen for my words to enter.

Next day mid-August 2012

I feel a sense of renewal this morning... the New Moon was last night—new beginnings! I am starting over now. I am choosing to be more conscious of what I eat, when I exercise, how my spiritual Self is feeling, and writing in journals and taking notes for when you connect with me.

My life is my own. I am the one who must decide how to move forward, to allow myself to heal in all ways, and to ask for guidance from my Higher Self. If I am to be here in the now, I must listen to the whispers and hear the words from within me. I allow myself to move forward with grace....

Are there any words for me today, David?

> Be silent... life is a reflection. What you intuit, you manifest. You know this; use it.
> Always with you,
> David

Next Day mid-August 2012

Since I am moving forward with this channeling, I sense you want to be with me each morning that I am home to send me information. I will sit here at the computer... close my eyes, and wait for your words to come to me.

> You asked about *heaven*. What you call *heaven* is like where you are. It is as beautiful as the hillsides of the mountains, soft as the oceans, and even more colorful than Earth. Heaven is just around the corner! You could touch me if you could only sense exactly where I am. Put out your arm and reach for me with your hand... I am here with you... whenever you need me, I am near you.

Why do I cry so often when I feel you are near me?

> I have learned that emotions travel faster than material energy.... Thoughts and emotions come to *heaven* instantaneously. We also generate energy or vibrations to reach you, which are instantaneous. There is but a thin veil or *energy vision* between where you are and where I am. Once I move from this energy level, I still will be able to visit you; however, just a portion of my energy will be with you. As I understand it so far, I will be able to separate into several energy levels, or tiers, to finish my education and teachings. Then when I am ready, I will be able to return to Earth, or other destinations. It is then that my energy as David will be put into my Record of Beings. I am still re-learning all these teachings from the high masters and Soul Beings. For now, I am here with you.
> Always with you,
> David

❧

I needed to take a reality break. Now with your photo near me, and a few channeling crystals perched in front of it, I am ready to receive more information about heaven.

What else can I tell you, I am here and you are there... a wink away from each other. When you lie down to sleep at night, I come and lay next to you. I touch your forehead and hold you tight. I know you feel me. This was part of the pact we made with each other. When you reached out a few moments ago, did you feel me?

Yes! Of course I did!

Barbara you have a sensing that anyone can have, but many do not wish to have... it is a sense-of-knowing, a sense-of-vision, and you have learned to intuit much that many cannot. That is why when we told each other that whoever leaves first must come back to tell the other of their experience, I knew I would be here and you would be there. You will share my words with others and a healing will begin for many.

It is easy for me now to see and sense-touch you... you and many others can do this too. This is why I am here to give you the insights from this *heaven* that you so want to understand.

As David, I always believed there was a heaven. Granny always taught that heaven was a holy place to hold the souls until other loved ones joined them.

[My phone rings...] That darn phone! Why didn't I think to turn it off? I will be sure to turn if off each time I sit to connect with you.

I ring the phone... sometimes when I want your attention, I ring the phone or the chimes in the backyard. I have learned how to connect with you in many ways, Barbara, so watch and listen for me in your days and nights.

Okay, honey, I will.... Bye for now.

Late August 2012

I am back.... Are you there?

I am always here with you, Barbara. Something you wish to know: It is okay with me that you are journaling my words, and whether they are for you only or for sharing with others. Everything here is open. It is not actually open, it just *Is*. If you can imagine a lightbulb and how turning it on creates light spreading outward from itself... that is how it is here. If I have a thought, share an opinion, ask a question, travel beyond your understanding to other places, reach out to sense-touch you, or separate my soul to seek another, all these actions become known to all. And, the same goes for all the other souls here. It is quite busy... no time for regrets, pity, or negative thinking because everyone is moving forward... toward their own unraveling of their soul's journey. Can you understand?

I think so. It sounds like that lightbulb is always on. That everyone emits a Light and it is moving forward because nothing moves backward, right? Also, you knew exactly what I was going to ask first!

Yes, Barbara. Souls are always moving toward their final destination—which is not really a destination, more of an envelopment into the Oneness. I know you know these things.... I will help you remember them. My Light is shining as yours is, except my Light here is a flow of energy that is considered my soul Light. Your Light in material form also comes from your soul, but it can get clouded when you become depressed, have negative emotions, or act in a less-than-positive response to your surroundings. What happens in your space-time to cloud your soul consciousness is an accumulation of many things; emotions, actions, reactions, others' actions and reactions, negative thoughts of fear and doubt. All these bring you to a place of diminished Light. When you are in a free and positive mode of emotion and wellbeing, you are emitting a true Light, just as I am here. Keep your Light, Barbara... just as in the song I sent you after I left, "Keep your happiness."

Thank you, honey....

Okay, I keep thinking I should keep writing today with you. What else can you share now?

What do you think when you think of *heaven*? Most likely, you think what I thought when I was in the physical world. I thought it was full of angels, clouds, a Super Being named God, and most of the things I was taught in church as a boy. Granny used to tell me heaven was like a peaceful place where souls could redeem their sins. Barbara, where I am, you can call heaven because there is no word for it here... it is just the Oneness. I will begin when I, the David you knew, left the Earth's plane of existence.

When I first realized I was *away* from my body was in my room in our house. I could see that I looked asleep, lying on my bed, very still. As I looked closer, I realized that that body was not *me*. I was above my body lying on the bed; I was looking down upon it. I realized then we truly are not our bodies. I was here... me... my body was there, limp and lifeless. I know it is hard for you to go back and think of that day again, Barbara... but I believe it is the right time for us to go through your questions and for me to share with you. I feel your energy is increasing with your spiritual exploration and understanding... into the realms of where I am... heaven. This is why I want to share my *Story of Heaven*. It is my gift to you.

I have so many questions honey—I don't know where to start!

There is no start, no beginning, and no ending. There is really only continuity, a continual stream of life. Life as a soul always is... life on a material plane can be chosen. When our Soul Being wishes to materialize into a life form, we take the time necessary to decide on many options we have in which to incarnate. I know you believe in reincarnation, Barbara... this is a truth. You have been incarnating for many lifetimes on Earth. I have been with you, as you know, for many of those incarnations. Our lifetimes together have been seeking our truth as humans, experiencing our *matas*, and following our chosen journeys. We have also had many incarnations throughout other realms. Those you will discover when you are here with me. It is then that we will study our incarnations to decide if we wish to choose another together.

Late August 2012

I feel you so close today, David... thank you for being here with me. My next question has to do with this journaling. Should I combine my entire journal writing for the past year, since you left, with this channeling from you?

As you read and write each day, you will select those parts to join together with this channeling. You will know what should be left out and what should be included. Your next book will contain your own creative writing... this journaling is from me to you. You are such a perfectionist! Trust yourself, Barbara; your writing touches many souls and has transformed more people than you could imagine. I honor you and your talents. I know you are a good storyteller and writer; now I want to be a part of that creativity with you.

David, you sound so different... you were not much of a talker. You were a very reflective man, I know that, but you didn't talk much to me, especially about your feelings. When you did share with me, you kept limits to just how much you would disclose. It is difficult to hear you talking so much now.

As David, I was created by the experiences I had as David. As a Soul Light, I have the range of many lifetimes, the intellect of many minds, the abilities of many experiences from which to draw. As I have said before, I am with the Oneness. You are with your individual knowledge—your life experiences, emotions, thoughts, and so forth. There is a limitation to the soul when incarnated into a life form. Where I am there are no limitations. I can use words beyond your vocabulary on Earth, say and do anything, go anywhere, and I am in the Oneness where all is open. You will get used to the way I sound and talk, Barbara; just keep typing.

Always with you...

Next Session: August 2012

You know me; I would like to be more organized with this channeling. Let me start with this simple question: Is it true that another soul meets you on the other side after you die?

Yes. There are souls that have the duty of meeting those appearing here. It is like a big train station... where those from other material realms appear in the Oneness. If there are no familiar souls right away to greet you; it is because those who want to meet you are without a tier, or layer of their soul, to appear before you. But soon after coming to the Oneness, each soul is given a type of orientation as to where they are, and soon they remember the familiar routine of it all, and the souls of loved ones appear.

Rich was here waiting for me, and soon I was able to connect with Granny, Shirley, Paul, and James. There was also a phantom soul; she was the one you were supposed to bring into our reality together. When we were living with your parents after I was drafted, she changed her direction for incarnating and you miscarried. She is a gentle soul that chose not to incarnate on Earth. All souls have the opportunity to experience this interruption, in some form; she chose to experience this with us. I know you will remember her when you join us here. Does that answer your question?

Yes. You had said you became aware that you were looking over your physical body in the bedroom; do souls fly?

> Flying is the term you use when you have a dream that you are up above the planet or out in the Earth's skies. Flying is not the word I would use... more like *appearing*. I appeared above my body and I appeared here. It is as if an *instant knowing* happens and I can be anywhere I desire. Once the initial, let me term it *downloading* because you will understand that terminology, is concluded, a soul can instantly be wherever they wish. This is so we can learn, grow, and decide what we want to do and where we want to experience our *matas* or lessons next. Of course, I am making it sound very simple... just so you can have a better awareness of it now.

You mention the term *downloading*, but you never learned to use my computer. How would you know to use that word?

> This term is what I use so you will grasp more of what I am telling you. Barbara, once a soul passes into the Oneness, we know whatever has been discovered, created, thought, experienced, and sensed. I am in the Oneness... the Divine Soul where all is known. You will remember many of the things I share with you and you will dream about them. You will have a greater understanding of your Soul Light and Soul Being as we communicate.
>
> Always with you....

Next Session: Late August 2012

Honey, you have come to me at a time I needed to be inspired— thank you!

You have talked about "a layer of your soul" or "connecting" with other "tiers." What do you mean?

> When a soul is in the Oneness, we can easily understand all the parts of a Soul Light. In heaven, a soul is fluid, or think of it as air... not bound by limits of physical boundaries. As I tell you more about the mystery of heaven, it will become more clear.
>
> Compare the explanation above to the details of a crystal... like many you possess. The crystallized form is always growing; it is a live, living entity. I know you know this. Each

tiny bit of crystallizing tier is an individual form of life; however, it is also a cumulative part of the whole crystal. This is also true of souls. When I am here with you, Barbara, I can also be in other realms of existence. My Soul Being, which is my soul's guide or caretaker, is made up of many souls that have their own experiences and their own lifetimes. Some of those lives are on Earth, some are not. You can compare a Soul Being to your Higher Self when incarnated.

When I appeared in heaven, I was only concerned with where David had been, how he lived, whom he loved, what accomplishments he had completed, and if he had learned the lessons, or *matas*, he had chosen. After several Earth months of *downloading*, I was shown the mystery of my Soul Being. Even now, I am learning many details. As I have said, David is still a part of my Soul Light, and always will be; it is not necessary to lose the memory of any lifetime. And when you dream about me, think about me, say my name, pray for me, meditate on our lives together, I will be there always. However, I have other lessons to learn, and in a chosen space, I will venture toward a new realm of soul experience. This is why many psychic mediums can focus on a soul who has passed into the Oneness... but as the soul begins to connect with their Soul Being, this becomes more faint.

You have a question....

Yes, there is so much to understand. You said you would wait for me to explore another life; now you say you will be going to learn other lessons. Will you be available for me when I pass over into the Oneness?

Yes, yes... I will be with you as you appear in the Oneness. I will always be with you, Barbara, as I have said. Perhaps I need to give you more of a mind-picture of the Oneness. Use your intuition to sense what I tell you.

I have re-learned, and quite easily upon returning to the Oneness, that our Soul Being is a group of soul energies. Each Soul Light energy has its own experiences, its own reflections of life forms lived in many realms. As the Soul Being experiences more and more realms of existence, it learns, grows, and becomes closer to all that *Is*... the Oneness. My life with you as Barbara was one of those lifetimes my Soul Being has experienced. My lifetime with you as Barbara has been one in which I have learned so much, and I am still learning as I explore each experience we had together. I am still in the downloading dimension of my learning about my life as David. This may take many Earth months or even years, or it can happen in an instant.

I can sense Rich's soul around me, he is venturing to other realms... but remember, a part of him can still be near you always. When he greeted me upon appearing in the Oneness, he was Rich, and then I realized only Light, as I was also a Soul Light before him. I know I am being transmuted into my Soul Being. This timespace we have together is to help you understand the *heaven* people on Earth so wish to learn about and to answer your questions about the lifetimes and matas we shared.

I need a break....

Okay, I am back. Let's see... you were telling me about how Soul Beings have many "parts or tiers" and can incarnate into several lifetimes or life forms at once, correct?

Yes, Barbara. Some on Earth know this. Most humans like to think that their life on Earth is the one and only one in which they, or their soul, experience. In actuality, each life form has a Soul Light, but that soul is one of many which make up their Soul Being. When we were together, you tried to tell me a bit about what your beliefs were and it was difficult for me to understand it all because I really thought that I, as David, was the only life my soul would experience. Now, here, it is clear that our Soul Beings have many experiences concurrently.

As you have learned, Barbara, there is not a timespan as you know it, so our lifetimes can be intermingled, or envisioned at once. As I become more aware of my connection within the Oneness, I can envision my lifetimes and life experiences, and realize how they all combine into the wholeness that is my Soul Being. Of course, there are levels, many levels of life experiences—do you follow?

Sort of....

There is much more to remember. It feels like I have always been here... even though I remember you and all our lifetimes together. I will be sharing some of these with you because you told me before I left that you wanted to write one last book about our many lives together, making it a memoir of lifetimes. I can help you with that book by telling you details about many of your soul's lifetimes spent with my Soul Light, and others you have loved.

I have another question: Can anyone contact a loved one on the other side to obtain all this information about heaven?

Yes, of course! Many humans have the ability to connect with souls in the Oneness. However, many do not truly want to do this... and many souls here do not want to be contacted. There is a shroud of mystery to the Oneness. If a soul wants their loved one to know them while here, there is a space when this can happen. I am in this space; this is why you can sense my words so clearly. If you would have tried to connect with me earlier, I would not have been available. As I have said, there is much downloading to do that interferes with the link of communication. Now, I am available to you and will stay with you until you feel completed in your questions. This is the pact we had talked about before I left. I am always with you, Barbara... only a thought, a whisper, a dream away.

Next Session:

So, being a channel or psychic medium is truly a valid experience, correct?

Yes. Remember when you took me to a few mediums who claimed to hear, sense, or see souls who had left Earth? I was very skeptical. Actually, there are many mediums who have these abilities... you are one of them. You have known this for a long time, but you were not quite ready to believe or use your talent. Now is the time to develop your channeling abilities, put your words in books, and help guide those on Earth who seek knowledge and healing. Many will follow your words... education is a bountiful endeavor. Use your teaching abilities through your writing.

If you wish to use my words in a storybook, that is fine too. Either way, more sensing of what heaven is will be transpired by those who seek to understand more clearly.

I need another break....☺

I have studied about many laws within the universe... are there such laws?

You know there are, Barbara. The laws within your universe are very clear to those who wish to know them. Many of these laws have been written about and shared for eons of your timespace. There are many laws: The Law of Karma, the Law of Birth into Being and Passing to the Oneness, the Law of TimeSpace, the Law of Expansion and Contraction, the Law of Free Will, the Law of Gravitation, the Law of Transmutation, and the Law of Soul Migration. All these and many more could be termed Earth's Universal Laws; however, many do not apply to other universes, and some pertain only to the Earth's galaxy. Each galaxy has its own set of galactic laws as well. There is a *system of universal action* that also takes place on Earth, as well as, other planets and/or other realms. All these laws and systems work concurrently and without effort—they just are and always will be.

As David, my limitations in understanding the life cycles, and even my own soul, kept me from understanding what now is a natural knowing. Remembering, or as we have termed it here, downloading the mystery of the Oneness is a joy. It is peaceful here, not like the unsettled Earth and other planets, which have a dense physical reality. I am David's soul, yet also joining with other levels, all within the scope of my Soul Being. If I focus on you and Earth, I sense your form and your soul. If I focus on my Soul Being, I sense activities of all sorts, some dense and some only Light or emanations of Light. It is most beautiful, Barbara... most beautiful.

I have to interrupt you because there is another family of deer settled outside my office window, under the big shade tree. A doe, two twin fawns, a young buck, and a large buck with a large rack. You know how much I appreciate living here, and I am so happy we moved here before you left. I feel your presence in the backyard every time I go outside and hear our wedding anniversary chimes ring their deep majestic sounds. I know there is a part of you here with me almost every day... I just wanted to say, "Thank you."

Now, new question: Do Earth's animals have souls too?

Animals surely have a form of soul, yes indeed. They float from incarnation to incarnation until there is a choice on some level to experience a higher level of physicality. So, as in many belief systems you have studied, animals are a natural progression of all life forms on Earth. This is occurring as well on many planets in other universes unknown to Earth. Soul Beings are only for a higher vibration of life form, such as humans and other physical life forms found in other universes. If your question is in reference to pets, like our dear Goldie and Tizzy, know that each life form has its own space in the Oneness.

When you came to the sacred spot on the walking trail just a few weeks after I left, you were correct in knowing that Rich, Goldie, and I were there waiting for you.

Oh yes! I sat down on that old fallen log and felt you and them so much. I cried and cried and felt yours and Rich's hand on each of my shoulders and Goldie's head between my knees. It was a magical reunion for me, David. Evidently, Goldie could reunite with us all at that time, which makes perfect sense to me.

There are so many questions! Can you enter my dreams?

When a human being is in a *dreamstate*, the super-conscious mind is resting in a higher vibration than when it is in a conscious state. Dreams come from a crossover between the conscious, subconscious, and the super-conscious states of awareness. In other words, dreams form in your brain and contain many images from your waking state, conscious memory; they can also join with images from the super-conscious, or Higher Self. *Dreams are a result of your brain's activity and your soul's sensitivity.* Some people dream only from their consciously active states of mind, bringing images and stories from their present or past experiences. Others dream from a more super-conscious state, which crosses over into the space of events that may not yet be experienced or envisioned.

When you were a young child, you were able to dream visions of events that had not yet taken place, these could be called what has been termed *prophetic dreams.* You still have these dreams, but many times choose on a higher level not to remember them when you awaken. If you focus your intuitive sensing on your dreams, you will have many questions answered, Barbara.

I visit you in your dreams when I feel it to be the most valuable to your understanding and comfort to do so. If you

want to have more joining with me in your dreams, ask before
you go to sleep and I will be there with you.

Always with you...

Next Session:

Fall will be here soon... help me to understand the concept of space
and time a bit. The concept of no space or time is still very difficult for
me to understand.

This is a difficult law to grasp when in a material body on
Earth. Let me explain it this way. Your mind is full of
memories from your life, and even some from other lifetimes,
and they all seem to flow from one to the other in a succession.
A *flowing of life* is how we can term this succession of
knowing, to better grasp the illusional concept of time.
Everything, living and nonliving, takes up space, even my Soul
Light. Space is energy. Energy is matter. When our souls
incarnate into a physical matter, they are bound in a sense of
density that flows very slowly; so slowly, one cannot see this
movement unless looking directly into the cellular level.

Matter, such as nonliving materials, flows even more slowly
and is set into form, changing only minutely. This would be
like what you consider Earth's rocks—although rocks are living
and changing. The progression continues in levels as in
crystalline forms. You can understand that during the different
seasons, plants on Earth, which are living forms, change in
their timespace because you can actually see them change as
they flow through their cycles. So, *time is matter moving ever
so slightly through space.*

Your timespace is set for Earth to explore karma, the cause
and effect law of many universes. To experience the results of
karma, there needs to be a type of time-sequence. Time is a
concept devised to assign order in your universe. Without the
concept of time, people on Earth would not be able to interpret
their behaviors, actions, and reactions. Without this
interpretation, there would be no societal constructs, human
compassion, or sense of structure within your existence. Time
is a necessary law of Earth just as the cycles of life are
necessary for people to learn, grow, and evolve. In actuality,
there is no time—*the Oneness is ever present, ever learning,
ever evolving concurrently.*

You talk freely about karma… it is a known law to most on Earth, but not everyone clearly understands it. Is it innate, even though many do not consciously understand it?

The word karma is a good term for all cycles of learning and for that which all incarnated forms experience. *Karma is a magical element of learning, growing, and evolving with the Oneness.* All Soul Lights flow in-and-out of incarnations, in-and-out of *matas*, reaching for continuance with the Oneness. And the Oneness is also flowing, evolving infinitely. It is the great mystery of existence.

All incarnated forms and souls have the seeds of knowing the laws of karma. It is up to them individually to learn and understand their karmic patterns in which to learn, grow, and evolve. *If a soul does not give attention to the seeds of karma, patterns are lost in a continual downward spiral. However, if one nourishes those seeds, they will learn their matas and progress toward a better understanding of their journey.* We are all on our own paths, individually guided by our souls and our Soul Being, both in material form and in the Oneness. Paths cross many times between those who are in a soul family such as you and I.

Karma has been depicted infinitely. Some believe in a karmic *debt*, while others sense karma as a form of repentance. As I have said, *karma is an action which reflects the magical element of learning, growing, and evolving with the Oneness.*

Next Session:

Hi, honey… looking at your photo and your deep penetrating eyes, I see so much more of who you were than I ever knew. I remember when that photo was taken. We were on our anniversary trip along the coast to Oregon. I am so glad we took that trip! It was a true bonding for us after our son's passing… we needed to re-group ourselves and our relationship.

I have a question about the "soul families" you spoke about earlier. How many souls does a Soul Being consist of, and are there other souls, which are a part of our soul family, that I know from this lifetime?

Since Soul Beings contain many souls, even I do not know all of them. I am learning that souls do group together many times, and incarnate into the same space-time in the same realm. This can be evidenced by the many human families that have incarnated for many generations. Sometimes, but not always, those who have incarnated with power, success, and royalty; poverty and war; identifying careers and dedications; or boundaries and territories, incarnate together to secure that distinction for each soul to experience the others. Doing this helps to ensure that those souls re-experience, perhaps many times, all the experiences and matas as a material form on Earth, and even in other realms.

We have experienced many lives together, but not with all the other souls in our soul family. Our lifetime included Rich, whom we have also had several lives with, and Cindy with whom we have had fewer lives together. Rich is from a different Soul Being and Cindy is from our own soul family. Also, within our soul family are many others we have incarnated together with as a group. We have had lives with all of these souls before, either knowing one another, or separately and not meeting physically in those lifetimes. There may be others whom I will learn about after joining with our Soul Being.

So, there are lessons we have to learn each time we incarnate into a material form—what is the purpose of these lessons, or matas?

Each incarnation manifests the Oneness. As souls, it is our desire to experience all that *Is*. In other words, we know it is our job, or duty, to grow and evolve within the Oneness; therefore, the Oneness evolves. Each Soul Light accepts it will experience as many lessons, or material and nonmaterial experiences, as possible to further the growth and evolution of the Oneness. Matas are the events, experiences, actions, reactions, thoughts, decisions, insights, and emotions in all situations, by all our material and nonmaterial life forms and realms of being that we choose to experience, which direct us toward the Oneness.

So, the Oneness, or God as many term Divine Energy, is also evolving as we evolve?

Yes. The word evolve is not a word chosen here but is a good one for you to understand the concept. All life is growing, or evolving, even the Oneness. The Oneness is merely energy, Light. I cannot see the Oneness as I see the Light-forms of souls in my Soul Being and other souls around me. The Oneness is *unsee-able*... but is *sense-able*. I *sense* the Oneness around and with me just as you sense God all around and in you. The Love of the Oneness has no boundaries, no restrictions, and no judgments.

Because the Oneness is all Love, there is no need to seek redemption for what our experiences are in an incarnation. *We incarnate to experience All That Is, and therefore, all that is experienced expands the Oneness.* The belief on Earth that one commits sins, and then needs to repent or seek redemption from a master, god, spiritual teacher, or God, is a *miss-take*. Each experience is a lesson, a learning experience to move you, your soul, forward on its journey. Even the experience of undergoing a trauma, physical or mental illness, or an injury is an opportunity for soul growth, which in turn supports the Oneness to evolve.

If one's actions and reactions cause harm to oneself or others while incarnated in a material form, the soul's growth is limiting its expansion, as it is limiting the expansion of its Soul Being, and the Oneness. Nothing is without cause and effect. Nothing is without loss and gain. Every thought, deed, word, action, or the receiving of these is not without repercussion for that action or reaction. Therefore, all life experience is valuable.

Would you say then that having an addiction to illicit drugs and/or alcohol while here on Earth is a manifestation of cause and effect, karma? And that such an addiction is limiting that soul's growth? Of course, these questions pertain to my interest in recovery addiction and our son's lifetime.

Basically, yes, to both questions, Barbara. An addiction is an outcry for love and direction on the human plane of existence, and at the same time, an *effect* of karma in which that soul needs to experience a counterbalance to another lifetime. Since our lifetimes are in actuality happening in a continual timespace, *one exact lifetime may or may not be a cause and one an effect.* There are gaps, *timespace spans,* that are not followed by an individual soul but by each Soul Being. Because of this, I cannot say if one of Rich's lifetimes was the result of some *cause* experienced in another—only our Soul Beings know these truths. I do understand that all experiences are valued and valid. As I have said, each experience of a life form in a lifetime is a lesson, a learning experience to move the soul forward on its journey.

There are many who believe having an addiction in a lifetime on Earth is one of the more difficult lives to experience; this would be because of the self-inflicting behaviors that are filled with mental and physical pain, depression, and unfavorable societal factors involved with the life of one addicted. It is important to remember that all souls will experience a lifetime with an addiction of one type or another. Have compassion for those who have chosen their current life experiences to include this experience, *for this is also a mata for you, the person in witness.* It would be less complicated if all life forms remembered that they have, or will experience, all situations in their cycle of lifetimes. If this would be possible, it would help counterbalance others to maintain a positive frame of reference when living with or loving one with an addiction, and all living forms in general.

Addictions to drugs and alcohol, especially on Earth, can be experienced on all levels: mental, physical, emotional, and spiritual. Some currently believe that one with an addiction is of a lesser state of spiritual evolvement. This is not so. Many who explore with drugs or alcohol on Earth are doing so to expand their consciousness, to widen their experience of being a part of the Oneness. The physical addiction begins much later than the inner spiritual quest for expansion. The mental functioning of the human brain is quite able to contain the expanded realms of being which activate spiritual expansion, but the physical Earth body cannot. In other life forms, the use of consciousness expanding substances is quite common.

Those souls who have experienced expanded consciousness on other realms of existence, and desire to experience it within a human body, do not have the physicality to experience it in the same manner. They become distraught and cannot understand why their bodies are not complying with their wish to sustain their connection with an expanding level of consciousness. Some never find their happiness with this type of life and choose to move forward on their journey, away from planet Earth, this is why Rich left so young.

Always with you…

Next Session:

Last night I couldn't sleep very well because of my back pain. While lying on the bed, I was thinking about this writing and how it could go into my book. It came to me that since you will be giving me information about our lifetimes together that will go into the book, your channeled words might be nice at the conclusion. Instead of making this a separate booklet on channeling, it could be placed at the end as a point of reference so readers would understand my quest for unraveling the mysteries of heaven. I will think about that possibility.

Now, let me ask another question: How is it that some people have more knowledge or insight as to the spiritual aspects of life, while others seem so blocked even to wanting to explore it?

As the poet Rumi whom you like so much, wrote, "Look for the answer inside your question." You know the answer to this question, Barbara. There is a range of knowledge and many levels of understanding within individual souls, therefore, life forms. Humans have the ability to learn any insight, spiritual law, universal law, galactic law, spiritual practice, belief system, and so forth that they wish. Each soul is stationed at its individual level of seeking and learning, either in conscious, subconscious, or super-conscious learning levels. The Oneness is open and can be reached and understood by all beings in all realms, if the desire is awakened.

Some life forms do not wish to explore all that *Is* because they have incarnated to learn other, more dense, experiences. In the Hindu religion, which you have studied, remember the levels of existence? You learned this religion when you were what they term a "householder" and were busy raising our family. So it is with the journey of all souls. Each soul has chosen to experience and learn certain lessons, *matas*. When a soul is busy learning and experiencing its mata, this is of primary regard. If one's mata is to be spiritually knowledgeable, then they will seek this source.

Most souls have many matas to experience in one lifetime, some include the studies of a spiritual nature and some do not. Your lifetime has been filled with many matas, Barbara, one of which is to learn the truth of your spiritual quest. As David, I was a large part of your householder stage of exploration; now your attention is turning more to understanding the Oneness and to sharing that knowledge. This is why I have decided to stay with you for this precious timespan—to help guide you.

I like the word "mata." It sounds like Mother; is there a connection?

The term refers to the teachings each soul must experience while on Earth. The Earth is Mother to all humans and as such holds all souls in compassion as they grow and learn. Another word you could find for Mother Earth's experiences is *amma*. Other planets, and non-physical realms, have their own terms for lessons experienced within their scope of existence. When one's matas on Earth have been explored in a lifetime, the soul moves back into the Oneness as I have done.

Please tell me about the masters.

The great masters of the Oneness are our Soul Beings. They do not incarnate into other realms; they do not incarnate at all; they just *are*. To understand the Soul Beings, Barbara, you would need to tap into your higher super-conscious mind, or higher soul-Self. Soul Beings keep the records of all the souls in their care. They are Light beams, or signals generated from the Oneness.

Think of that lightbulb again; visualize the bulb as a Soul Being and all the light beams from it as their souls in-keeping. The souls venture outward to land on many individual places, emitting the Light from the bulb. And the bulb, the Soul Being, is connected to the Oneness—the Divine Power Source.

As for the *masters* who have incarnated into life forms, they have, and are, radiating beams of Light, just as you and all other life forms are. Humans love to have labels for everything; they are a very organized group of beings. You label humans as teachers and masters who have completed their matas and have shared their knowledge with others. Those you call masters have been or are human beings, and other life forms on other realms, who have accomplished their chosen journey's matas. There have been and are many masters on Earth. This is evidenced by soul progression, entering the levels of higher knowing and being. Enveloped in the Oneness, they transmute all that *Is*. Many of Earth's masters will no longer incarnate; they will stay with the Oneness infinitely.

I want you to realize that what I am transferring to you is

coming from my knowledge as a Soul Light, and each time I share with you, I am becoming more connected with my Soul Being. As I re-learn the vast knowledge of the Oneness, I will join with other souls from our Soul Being and incorporate their knowledge and life experiences; they are infused with my own.

You may have noticed how my sharing is changing; it is the result of an expansion of my soul, and I feel further from the person, David, whom I was in our lifetime together. Please try to understand that I am no longer *I* but *We*. When I, as David, want to remember my time with you as Barbara, I can do so, but my language is changing to include my Soul Being, and all of its souls.

I think I am beginning to understand... you are becoming a part of the soul family, right? And as this happens, you become more and more aware of the other souls and all their experiences and knowledge.

Yes, that is it exactly. After much downloading and re-examining of a lifetime, we recount, uncover, or discover the Oneness again. When this happens, the lifetime begins to fade and we are rejoined with our soul family. We can intuit each other's experiences, download their knowledge which was learned in other lifetimes, and grow closer in the Oneness. There are many lifetimes before us, some we have experienced. This would be a good step in sharing with you about those lifetimes our souls have shared together. You have remembered some in meditations, dreams, and visions. When you want to begin, let us know.

Next Session:

I have a few more questions I would like to ask before I begin to write about our lifetimes, is that okay?

Yes, Barbara. What are your questions?

You were telling me about the masters on Earth, and other realms, and how they join with the Oneness when they have finished their lessons. Specifically, I would like to know about a few of the men we call spiritual masters who have lived on Earth. First, what can you tell me about Babaji?

You ask about Babaji, but you already know him, Barbara. You have been drawn to him this entire lifetime and in other lifetimes as well. Babaji is a High Master known to all on many realms of existence. He can and has incarnated at will in any stage of his ageless form on many occasions. Babaji is a bringer of peace and compassion to all realms of existence. If you but meditate on his Love, he will be there for you just as we will always be with you when you ask.

And can you tell me about Jesus of Nazareth? Will he return to Earth?

Again, Barbara, you know him well. Jesus has been and always will be a High Master of Light emanating his truth and goodness whenever called upon. He lived and died in a glory revealed by his presence of Love. He was a man, as well as incarnated forms in other realms. He is, as is Babaji, joined with the Oneness and will not return to Earth or other physical realms.

Most on Earth name a spiritual teacher a *master* when they have chosen to incarnate to expand the Oneness at an accelerated speed, which in turn guides the universe toward a higher energy vibration and evolution. Some masters are living on Earth presently, and there will be other masters to join Earth as long as Earth lives; this is the way of the evolvement of humanity.

The master teachers are held in highest honor by all souls for they have experienced enlightenment of the Oneness and shared that knowledge with others while incarnated in many life forms. There have been many masters incarnated on Earth, who may not be known to many, but their powerful Light can be felt both globally and throughout many universes. There are also many master teachers who have lived on Earth, or are still living on Earth, which many recognize. These include the many successions of the Dalai Lama, Gautama Buddha, Paramahansa Yogananda, Vistar, Aurobindo, Mahatma Gandhi, Mother Teresa, Baha'uliah, Sai Baba, as well as, many others.

Who is Vistar? I have not heard that name.

The prophet Vistar's last incarnation upon Earth was a million Earth years ago. He attempted to bring the concept of compassion to humans. He ventured from another galaxy to touch the souls on Earth, providing them with an increase in intellect and Love. He was chosen to accomplish a mata rare among humans, that of securing a rite of passage from one age of existence to another. His soul is also with the Oneness and will not incarnate again.

What can you tell me about angels?

What you term as *angels* are in fact beings of Light that choose not to incarnate into life forms of any kind. They are like messengers from the Oneness which can choose to stay near and help guide others on many realms of existence. The depictions of angels flying around with wings that Earth's artists have rendered are somewhat accurate. Angels hover at a high vibration and can *translocate*, as souls can. They do not have wings as you envision it. The name *angel* comes from the term *angelic*, which speaks of the Oneness. Angels are real in the sense that they have an impact on all beings.

Many angels choose to remain close to only a few life forms for their entire lifetime, while others choose to emit their guiding Light toward groups of beings. Many humans have been able to sense the angels around them or others. This sensing can be shared by holding the hand of the one intuiting. Another method to sense the angels is to sit in silence, ask for direction from your angels, and intuit your visions. These beings of Light will always be with you, Barbara; they can easily be sensed; just envision them.

Please explain why we cannot remember all of our lifetimes.

The incarnated forms a soul chooses to take are not a secret to you or other beings; however, if you could actually remember the many lifetimes you have experienced, it would bring you to a point of confusion. Your mind could not be in peace where you are presently if you knew every experience you have had as life forms on many realms. Many can remember, or pull from their super-conscious, a few lifetimes, usually on Earth, to receive glimpses of their soul's incarnations. Even in dreamstates, or deep meditation, some have envisioned incarnations of their soul. You will recognize all your incarnations, just as I do, when you are once again in the Oneness.

All incarnations are recorded in a type of Hall. Our Soul Beings have access to these records and use them to instruct souls on their journeys. On Earth, people have termed these records the Akashic Records; this is a good term, for it implies the *ethereal records*. The records are not actually physically written; they are *imprinted thought forms*. These thought forms are the entire compass of experiences of all souls and are the power, or motivation, for the Oneness to continue evolvement. Some on Earth have tapped into these records through deep contemplation on the Oneness, but no one life form has access to the entire Hall of Records.

Can you explain why there is so much violence on Earth?

Of course you would ask this question, Barbara; you understand that you, your soul, came from a center of peace and Light. For those who remember what the Oneness is, it is more difficult to tolerate the violence found in many realms of existence. If you think back on all we have told you so far about souls incarnating to experience *all life experiences*, you can understand why it is necessary for some to experience lifetimes of violence and some to be present while violence is occurring. Earth has always been a disruptive planet, but one where a quickened evolution can, and is, taking place. Other planets and realms have less violence and a slower vibration of energy.

Many on Earth choose lifetimes to experience the dense base emotions of aggression. It has always been evident that Earth can provide souls the engagement of base emotions such anger, aggression, jealousy, and destruction toward others, but within an accelerated pace of evolution. These lessons are usually learned in a few lifetimes while on Earth, however, some souls have gravitated to experience them many times and have incarnated specifically to experience disruptive behavior; many have been in a succession of Earth's war experiences.

So, souls can choose to incarnate to experience specific physical and material pleasures, careers, talents, etc.?

Yes. All souls, with the guidance of their Soul Beings, have choices with regard to their choosing lifetimes and/or life forms. Some choose to experience that which *is the best mata for them to* expand on certain levels, while others deliberate on several choices. Once in the Oneness, we have the ability to re-learn and remember our soul's progression; from that place of knowing, we are offered many choices to explore. Depending upon whether we desire to progress with other souls within or outside of our soul family, we choose possibilities of lifetimes in which to return to Earth or other realms.

Each soul has progressed on its individual paths within its Soul Being, allowing it and its Soul Being to evolve. At this point we know of many lifetimes experienced on Earth with and without you. We would like to wait for you to appear back in our soul family before looking at the choices we will be offered with or without experiencing a lifetime with your Soul Light. When a soul is offered choices, it is a very intricate journey and not to be taken lightly. However, all lifetimes are an indication of great dedication to expand the Oneness and are highly rewarded.

Next Session:

As I understand it then, a soul can choose from "offerings" of different lifetimes with different experiences and lessons to learn?

Yes. The offerings are not as exact as some on Earth believe. Each lifetime is not chosen and then unfolds before a soul for approval, because that would suggest that lifetimes are predestined or laid out before them. Rather, matas are offered the soul, which will guide it toward a higher understanding of learning, growth, and illumination. Many factors come into play when choosing a lifetime and life form. Sometimes, more specific details can be offered surrounding the general experiences that will come into play during the soul's journey. Usually, there are offerings of incarnations that provide many matas for the soul.

If a soul desires to incarnate with another specific soul, or souls, that wish is highly considered, as is the desire for a journey surrounding a more specific life experience. On Earth that might include being an artist, dancer, teacher, spiritual teacher, laborer, psychic, soldier, and so forth. Also to be considered would be the gender the soul will inhabit, and to a smaller degree, the options of ethnicity, parents, siblings, and demographics. As you can imagine, to incarnate is a more complicated choice than most on Earth believe it to be, among those who have a belief system that includes reincarnation. It is to be noted again that the Oneness envelops the experiences and matas shared by all souls expanding infinitely.

As each soul and its Soul Being discover which matas they

wish to experience, review the Hall of Records and choose from the offers before them, they are ready for an incarnation birth. However, before a soul can incarnate, it must relearn, or remember, the Oneness and its infiniteness. In Earth time, this could be years or decades; a quick turnaround into an incarnation usually does not happen, although there are exceptions. Most souls choose to experience life forms on other planes of existence before returning to one such as on Earth.

Let me see; what other questions do I have for you? You had mentioned that there is a window of space now that you can come into my mind easily; will this opportunity be over soon?

Remember, Barbara; we will always be with you; however, now when your mind-frame is in high energy and you have a great passion for learning, we are here to help guide you toward a better understanding of heaven. You may use all or none of these words to share with others. Our limitations are few, but we do move forward also, to learn, re-learn, and become more complete with our own Soul Light and Soul Being. We can divide our energy to be with you more easily now rather than in another space when your energy levels may not be as receptive. You will receive all the information you desire to complete your book. Do you want to move forward into that area?

I guess I am not ready to start on my book yet; I am enjoying our connection on a more intimate level right now. Another question: What do you spiritually know now that you did not grasp or understand as David?

A very good question, Barbara. There is much realization that comes with appearing in the Oneness! We have re-learned that our spiritual connection to the Oneness was, is, and will always be. Among all life forms, within all universes, there is Love. Love is all that *Is* and will forever *Be*. Looking at individual life forms and tagging them good, bad, evil, spiritual, enlightened, and so forth is unwarranted, for all are equal. All life, material and nonmaterial, brings illumination to the Oneness.

There is much inequality of beings on Earth. It is common for one group of people to realize wrongly that they are superior or better than another group, or, to believe this on an individual basis. This is not Truth. We talked of violence and its necessity on Earth. Many humans have an innate knowledge of inequality; this is ingrained within them so they can complete their matas of violence and disruption. Those who have completed this mata in prior lifetimes usually do not readily comprehend the concept of violence currently.

We have learned that while in material form, it is most difficult to understand the complexities of the Oneness. There is no past, present, or future within the Oneness. Many humans have the ability to go deep within to connect with this High Divine Self to experience briefly this Truth: *There is only existence in the eternal Now. There arises a true perception of the infinite worth of that which Is when all preconceived birthrights, material manifestations, and thoughts of finiteness are surrendered. Nothing is or ever will reach finitehood. All is growing, all is evolving, all is within the Oneness of infinity.*

When we speak of eternity, your thoughts go to living beyond all time, correct? But *eternity is immeasurable; therefore, it does not begin, it goes nowhere, and does not end.* If eternity went beyond all time, that would be to say that at the end of time, eternity stops. So you see, one cannot use a timeline, or any measurable quantity to comprehend eternity. As the Earth expands and evolves, more insight will be given about the unknowable expansion of all the Universes. We say *Universes*, for they are immeasurable, just as the Oneness is.

We are learning that the evolution of humankind on Earth is accelerating in energy vibration, which is to say, one entering an incarnation on Earth can expand in ways never before experienced. A realization of sorts within each soul's awareness presently on Earth is attuned to a greater understanding of the Oneness, without the need for human saviors, avatars, or gurus to guide them. There is an individual innate draw toward deeply experiencing the Oneness within and around them. You have been connecting with all that *Is* for many lifetimes and can share your knowledge with others, if desired.

We are re-learning that when souls reappear in the Oneness, they are unaware, for the most part, of their inclusion in this infinity. Again, whatever a soul experiences in a lifetime is slowly passed through a filter of memory, then released as a faint thought. We are nearing the understanding of this now. In order for us to move forward on our soul journey, we allow the Oneness to enter our energy, our Soul Light, and we will drift toward a new expression of who we are. Soon, we must attend to our companion souls, finish downloading our life as David, and join our Soul Being. It is time for us to share with you some of the incarnations we have shared.

I have some questions first about our life this time, and our kids, and other things I am just curious about. Why did you need to leave this life so early?

As David, we did not decide to leave, but our Soul Light knew it was necessary. As David's Soul Light, which is communicating with you now, learned more of why he wanted to experience this lifetime, he knew there would also be an end to it. On this higher level, he knew there was so much more for him to do, especially with helping others. David became quite the person-of-service your last few years together, and this inspired him. Therefore, on a higher level, it was a choice to join the Oneness to seek other directions where his Soul Light could be of service.

We are now becoming more... integrated. Within this transition come the opportunities to expand, to evolve. This is our direction currently.

Do we, as humans, have the ability to choose our time to leave our bodies?

As we have shared, on a very high level, yes. But, this is not a human conscious decision. When humans do want to end their incarnations on Earth and rejoin the Oneness, there is a connection with their Soul Being which can be summoned to help guide in that direction, even in the matter of choosing to take one's own life.

Do you have an idea how long it will be before I join you?

Your lifespan as Barbara is a long and progressive one. You will have many more experiences with which to help expand your Soul Light and the Oneness. It is not for us to know when you will join us.

I feel so honored to be able to connect with you, David; you are now sounding like a teacher to me. Is there still time for me to get information about our lifetimes together for my book?

Remember, Barbara; we will always be with you on some level. It may not be this channeling we are pursuing, but if you desire more communication, always we will be with you. David's soul has now joined our soul family. We are here to guide you with your wishes for answers.

Can you tell me more of why Rich left so young? Did he take his own life?

His soul, as Richard, was re-experiencing a common thread of existence in a human body, that of addiction. Souls gravitate toward certain experiences in succession to grasp fully a mata. Rich's mata was again that of working the human body/mind addiction mata. We sense that he *was very prepared to leave his body* when he did, and is already connecting to another incarnation.

Our time with you and him may have been brief, but we surmounted many matas together. We have experienced many incarnations in this *trinity of souls*, like we just experienced. Some of these lifetimes we will share when you are ready to write.

Why have I felt such a great sense of loss most of my life? It seems to be a theme in my life.

Barbara... loss is a great awakening lesson. Loss has been in your life for many purposes. You are a beacon of Light on how to deal with loss... others follow your lead. When you react to loss, there is a factor you must consider—*nothing is lost*. On Earth, there is a field of reality that says, "Pain must follow loss." This is a human quality developed over eons of Earth time. In the beginning, people did not react so to their loss of another, or of things. As the Earth evolved, humans' emotional state needed to experience the cycle of all feelings. One of these is the feeling of losing someone close, or losing a material item of great value to them. Loss is merely a feeling; remember, you can control your emotions, Barbara.

After the passing of David, you felt a terrible loss... but now the loss emotion is not so strong. You have developed your life into a natural functioning pattern... a pattern without some of those you have loved, who have passed to the Oneness. Your ability as a human being is to allow yourself the feelings, the emotions you have... study them, feel them, and allow yourself to release those emotions that no longer serve you. Hold your feelings to you now; experience them, study them, and then allow yourself the gift of releasing what you no longer need as your lifetime progresses.

Always with you...

I am about ready to write, at least get information from you. I am hoping what you give me will be details of lives I know about from my own explorations, dreams, meditations, and visions. Also, please share with me those lifetimes I may need to learn from to further my spiritual understanding.

You must be clear when you begin. Wait until your mind is free of clutter and thoughts of questions about our words. You need to be further into your balancing of body/mind/spirit. Do your business of living and come to us at a later moment.

Always with you...

Channeling of Lifetimes

Fall/Winter 2012

Are you there? I need to hear your voice again, to hear your words in my mind.

> Clear your thoughts, Barbara; we are here for you always. Our time together on Earth was short, but you will always hear our words.
>
> You want to know more about our lifetimes together. Our lives have continued with the progression of many matas. We have learned, grown, and evolved many times together. Our lifetimes are recorded for us to sense.... When you return, we would like to experience yet another lifetime with you. If you are willing... we will continue our matas together.
>
> Learn to become more relaxed with your typing and let our words flow in your mind as your fingers touch the keys. No need to edit or rewrite a word... we are here to guide them. We are here to guide your thoughts to our lifetimes together as you wish to write them down. Are you ready?

Yes.

> We start with a lifetime together as sisters in the period on Earth called the *latent period of existence*. It was a hard time for the Earth and all upon it. It was an existence of fortitude, strength of body, and a love between us as strong as the rivers that flowed and the animals that roamed the land. Very young, we were thrown from a cluster of humans into a desolate terrain to tend to the duties of finding and bringing food to the group. We gathered roots, nuts, water, leaves, and herbs. We

slept arm-in-arm to stay warm and walked the land together until we could carry no more. Then we would return with our goods to share with the band of people in which we were born. We lived and died together in each other's arms, living only a short lifespan. This life was a learning lifetime of the mata *strength in body and mind.*

This is a lovely beginning to share with me of our lifetimes together. I can picture us as sisters, young and strong in body. The "latent period of existence" must be in the very beginning of Earth's time. Thank you so much....

✌

Late Winter 2012

What can you tell me about the life I had in 1500 BC? I remember telling you about my visions of being a Nubian princess who was taken from her tribe by Egyptians. I had not heard of the word concubine when I received this vision in the 1980s. I looked up the time period in two encyclopedias and found the exact lifetime and I was so excited. I would love to know more about this lifetime and if I received the details as they truly were. Can you tell me more about it?

This lifetime is one when David and Rich's souls were with yours again. The Egyptian Dynasty XVIII reigned during a traumatic yet progressive life. Our soul matas were of revenge for Rich, and trust for you during this lifetime. As you recount from your meditations, you were a truly rare beauty raised in the Nubian Desert in the Sudan of northern Africa. Your people were peaceful and had a lovely way about them, one of friendship and brotherhood. Your people treasured you as a young princess to their Chief Kabin. When you were abducted, you were about fifteen years old and not even aware of the civilizations in North Egypt. Your Nubian people worshipped the goddess Isis, whose cult was brought into their tribal territory from southern Egyptian lands, and you were named after her, Iset translating to Isis.

During the time ruled by king Thutmose, there was peace in the land of Egypt because he had conquered so much territory. It was not until that king or pharaoh died and his son became Egypt's ruler that war and terror came to the land of the gods. As a ruler, he was full of vengeance which was spurred by his wife and half-sister, who led him to conquer many lands with horrific methods. In contrast, his son was a great leader who also reigned beside his stepmother in the first several years as he became a man. He then became Egypt's head of armies and conquered many lands for Egypt, including miles down the Nile River into the Nubian Desert. However, this was done with respect and peaceful means, for his own mother, Iset, was from this Nubian land.

Born in the Nubian Desert of the Fifth Cataract called Barbar, Iset was destined to be a princess, for her father and mother had become royalty in their tribe. You were named Iset because your mother had a fondness for the Egyptian goddess Isis, who was introduced to her from the region of South Egypt. Living by the Nile River in the Sudan region was like living in a paradise. There were lush jungles, fresh clean water from the river, and plenty of vegetation and wild life to eat.

When the Egyptian army, instructed by Thutmose II, came to the land of Barbar, Iset was taken as a slave for the king. He chose her as a favorite slave consort, which led to her becoming his royal secondary-wife. That union produced a son and heir to the throne whose reign became famous for his many conquests of the surrounding lands. He ruled for many years with a gentle hand and was regarded as very popular by the people of Egypt.

This lifetime was a *soul trine*: You were Isis; Rich was Thutmose II; and, David was Isis' lover and head guard to the king, Gombat. This lifetime for us was one marked with deep love on all levels, but also jealousy and revenge. We lived and survived in a period of great differences between people and cultures; however, we accepted each other's position and rank. When Thutmose II died, Isis and Gombat were placed alive in his tomb with his wrapped body to die beside him, which was thought to ensure the souls' meeting again in the afterlife. This lifetime was very prominent in our souls' evolution in a trinity of learning matas together.

Winter 2013

The holidays are over—I missed you again. I am ready to hear more about our lifetimes now.

There is one lifetime we shared in which our matas were

chosen to be the same. It is of being together on a farm land. Rich green hills lining a somewhat barren land, we were together again our entire lives and that is all that mattered to us. We were young and experienced a challenging life of hard work. But, we had each other and were deeply in love. Much like all the lives we experienced together, we loved each other's souls, and could see our souls in each other's eyes.

This lifetime together came when there were wars and much hardship, but we were out of its harm. We were alone. We lived into our twenties together until the wars came to our land. We were slain. We were slain together and reached our soul family together.

Can you tell me in Earth time when this was and the location of this lifetime?

We were together in the early American colonies. The wars were of natives fighting for their land. We did not understand because we thought our land was *our* land. But the natives came to take their land and we were slain.

This sounds like our Earth time of the early settlers in America. I would guess somewhere in the early 1600s or 1700s, but I will need to look up history dates. Was I the woman again? What were our names? Can you tell me the period of time?

We were so close in this life and it is one of our favorite reflections with you. Yes, you were a female and we the male. Your name was Anna Jo and ours was James. We were about fifteen years old when we married. We rode horses and had a buggy filled with our belongings and traveled west from the Virginia settlement in the Americas. The time period was 1675 to the early 1700s. Our life together in the beginning was filled with hard work. We were so much in love we seemed not to let anything bother us... the soil was good and we planted our food, which was all we needed. James hunted for meat and stored it in a shed with salt. The nearest town was miles away and there would be many seasons that passed that we would not see anyone.

This lifetime was most difficult when the Americas and the natives fought for their land. We did not understand why we heard of land being taken away and given to the natives, or worse, when the natives just killed many who settled on *their* land. In the end, Anna Jo and James were raided by natives and their lives were taken. Our time together may have been short, but our hearts were cemented strong in this lifetime and we decided once again to enter Earth to experience other matas together.

Were any of our family members in this lifetime with us in that one?

The mother you know as Granny, who was David's mother; she was also James' mother in this early American lifetime. She was a robust woman in both lifetimes, always looking after others. When we moved west to find our own land, her heart was broken and she died soon after. Her name was June Ann Livingston and she lived her adult life in Virginia; her parents had come from England. Rich was one of the young Chickasaw braves who raided and destroyed our land; our deaths were not by his hand.

Can you tell me what we looked like?

Anna Jo was a few months younger than James and had blond hair with a fair complexion—as you do now, Barbara. However, Anna Jo was much larger than you and full of strength. She could lift as much as James and helped with many things usually left to men. James was small physically, but muscular and strong. He was dark in complexion with dark eyes and hair. James and Anna Jo knew they were to be together very young—about five or six years old. As children, they did everything together: fished, told stories, took long walks, ran fast, and played each day. They lived close, their homes were part of a group of small homes built for those who needed shelter but could not afford to buy land. The homes were part of a *governmental planship* for those who qualified. Their parents both qualified because James' mother was a widow and Anna Jo's father was a widower. They were among many who had this opportunity for governmental support to encourage the settlements of the Americas.

Your full name was Anna Jo Brackston and you were the only child of John Brackston, a stable owner. Your mother died giving birth to you, so you never knew her. You knew only a strong male influence through your father and learned many chores and things little girls were not exposed to, like shoveling and digging, fishing, building, and taking care of animals in the stable. The Brackstons were a hearty group of people who came originally to the Americas from Germany. There were many of German descent in the settlement of Virginia.

❧

Next Session:

I know you are near me--I feel you. I am probably too eager to learn more about my lifetimes spent with my family, but I am ready... are you there?

Always near you, Barbara, when you whisper. Your lifetime with Rich's and our soul as Native Americans was gracious and peaceful until the settlers arrived from the East. We shared several lifetimes together in the middle of the nation now called America. In most of these lifetimes we were very close. In one such lifetime, we were a woman and you were a male child of mine, as was Cindy, in this lifetime. We lived in the territory of the Dakotas. This lifetime taught us much about coping with the cold weather, the blessings of nature, and staying at one with the Great Spirit. We lived together in a small tepee without a man to guide us except for the tribal elders. You both were strong boys... you cared for us our entire life.

Also, you and Rich's soul had one very potent lifetime together as a warrior and his squaw. You were his wife, bearing many babies; we were one of those children. Rich was a brave warrior fighting in many tribal wars between the Cheyenne and the Dakotas.

What were the main matas during these Native American lifetimes?

Fortitude and strength of character. Living as natives, we experienced matas of learning about the land, nurturing one another, and growing in nature. When the settlers came into our land, the matas of the natives changed to ones of emotion. This was new to those who lived in the peace and love of the Great Spirit... Oneness. There was strife and war between men... causing many separations between tribes and families. The theme was much like the lifetimes of warriors in Asia, and of the Romans. Earth has been and always will be a land to learn about the hardships and suffering one can experience. If a soul chooses to be a human being on Earth, such lifetimes are a necessary part of evolvement.

❧

What can you tell me of the lifetime I know a little about between Rich and I as sisters in ancient times. I remember sharing it with you many years ago but it is a vague memory with little details.

You know this lifetime, Barbara. You shared it with me when it came to you in a meditation. It is of you and Rich's soul living in Asia Minor as sisters. You were the older, about thirteen or fourteen years old. One day as you both were walking, mounted Celtic warriors rode by on their horses. They were in their dress of helmets, spears, and swords. As they approached, they slowed and then stopped next to you. You and your sister bowed down immediately in respect as you were taught. Bowing your heads, you kneeled frozen in movement, with eyes lowered to the ground. One of the men said to another, "I want *that* one." He pointed to your sister. In an instant, the man who was spoken to started to jump off his steed, but before he reached you, your sister quickly took something out of her robes and swallowed it. By the time the man reached your side, your sister had died in your arms.

In this period, it was common for warriors to take young girls for their consorts to roam with the mounts of war from land to land. Your sister knew what was to become of her if they took her away and made the choice to end her life. You would have done the same if they had chosen you; your heart was lost when your sister died. You never recovered from this loss and became fragile and died at a young age for that period. Rich was your younger sister in this lifetime.

The bond between Rich's soul and your own has been strong, as strong as yours and mine. In this lifetime, you felt guilty for not being able to stand up and tell the warrior to take you, for your sister was too young. The fact that you could not *save* her has been traced into your current lifetime with what you went through with Richie's alcoholism. This mata has been repeated many times—learning that *one cannot save another from their chosen destiny.*

Each life is an individual experience of accumulated matas over many lifetimes. One's choices determine their path and the journey in which they are to evolve. Saving Rich's soul, as your sister in the lifetime in 300 BC, could not manifest, just as your saving him from his addictive choices in your current lifetime, could not transpire. Any traces of guilt you now own, if released, will detour another lifetime of this mata with Rich's soul.

Being so close to you through this communication is a dream come true, and I don't want to move forward, away from it and you. Let's look at another lifetime... perhaps my last one which I also know a bit about through meditations and dreams. It was my last lifetime before this one.

With a heart of a dove, you were a very special woman in a lifetime where we also played a role. It is also one in which you were given some insight within a vision you had many years ago. It was your lifetime before this one, during the great Earthquake of 1906 in San Francisco. Do some research on it and you will find a lovely woman in her thirties, elegant, gracious, and educated for that period. She gave birth to a son, but he was hidden from the local society in another location. They were so close yet lived far from each other. They would write and dream of a time when they could live closer, but that time never came.

You lived in the city in a small top floor bungalow with a long steep staircase. When the earthquake happened, you were trapped on that top floor. You tried to go down the stairwell, but the lower levels were already in flames. The flames were all encompassing and you could not get out. We, as your young child William, had our heart broken when we heard the news of our mother's death. The love we shared for each other as mother and child was deep, but the life together had the mata of an uncompleted life, much like many others we have shared.

I will research the earthquake in San Francisco... can you give me a name and what form of occupation she had?

Your name was Carrie Anna Williamson. She schooled in the art of medicine at the time in Earth's history when women were not socially accepted to be doctors. She treated those who were directed to her care through others who were fortunate enough to meet her and receive her healing touch. Carrie was a tall woman with thin frame, dark hair and eyes, and considered quite beautiful in that period on Earth. Her touch was as light as her voice. Her father was a medical doctor and she had the advantage of learning much in this area while growing up.

Her father, Dr. John Williamson, was a respected doctor in San Francisco. He was married to June Anna Evington, who also grew up in that city with very prominent parents.

Okay, I am really curious if any of the people in that lifetime were also souls from my current lifetime?

Yes, Barbara, we were together in that lifetime as mother and son. You were a beautiful young woman in that lifetime and very strong-minded. Your father being a prominent medical doctor, along with your well-known mother, guided you toward freedom in speech and in whatever you chose to pursue. As I said, women were not thought of as the right material to become a doctor in those times, but you were persistent and entered San Francisco's prestigious school of medicine.

It was in your second year of studies that you were sexually taken advantage of by a fellow student you knew only casually and became pregnant with your son. You did not tell the young man or anyone, except your parents, that you were pregnant. You were able to keep it a secret for long into the pregnancy, and when the time came to give birth, your father was there. He took you to another state to give birth, where there were relatives of the family. After your son was born, it was suggested by your father, and your mother agreed, that you could not pursue your studies and obtain your goal of becoming a doctor while raising a child. Also, at those times it was very unacceptable to have a child out-of-wedlock, so the child was adopted by the family relatives, the Muirs. You continued your studies for several more years.

Your father in this lifetime was your current sister's soul, Nancy. Your mother was Cindy's soul. The young man who was the father of your son was Rich's soul. And, as I said, we were your son, William. He was born prematurely and was not a healthy child. He lived most of his life in the Midwest with his adoptive parents and given their surname. After your death in the horrible earthquake in San Francisco, William's family moved to that city because he insisted he needed to be near where you lived and died. He died as a young man, about ten years after their move.

Did Carrie finish with medical school and become a doctor?

Carrie did not complete medical school; however, she schooled in other medicinal-type fields of which she knew instinctively and used naturalistic healing methods. Her practice became where her neighbors and friends lived, for she would go from home to home with her healing tools. She used herbs, tinctures, teas, and other medicinal modes. Barbara, your healing abilities have come from many lifetimes of working with nature's healing gifts. This is why during your current life, there was an innate goal to complete your schooling and use your abilities to heal others physically, psychologically, psychically, and spiritually. Your lifetimes on Earth have always included matas of learning and mastering the healing arts.

Next Session:

Tell me more about our lifetime together in Atlantis. Lazaris, the entity who has been channeled by Jach Pursel since the 1970s, shared with me during a reading in 1977 about this lifetime together with you. I would like to have more information.

Atlantis existed and its civilization was formed by those not from Earth's galaxy. These beings were heart-Lights who desired to traverse to new worlds to guide others to live in peace and love. They were large beings with high intellect who had the ability to use their minds to produce everything they needed or desired. They saw a struggling settlement on earth using twigs and sticks to form huts in which to live. They witnessed caring beings who lived a physically difficult form of life and decided to visit to teach them the ways in which they could learn and use their minds to manifest their needs. Many in the settlement did learn to manipulate their environments with their minds, while most of the others followed those who did. The settlers on Earth formed groups of those who could use their minds to create and manifest, and those who could not. This is when the visiting beings left, giving the name Atlantis to those who inhabited the island.

Atlantis became a highly trained, smooth-running civilization of people for many generations. However, the division of labor became too one-sided for those without the use of mind-power. They began to gather and learn about the powers of the cave crystals. This group fled to the caves of the hills when the great division occurred. The mind-dwellers lived in structures made of rock, marble, and stone in the valley. There were ornate pyramids developed through the use of their learned powers of mind manipulation, while the subservient group of people lived in the surrounding hills in caves.

Through the generations, the group of cave-dwellers taught themselves the powers of the many crystals found in the caverns of the caves. Soon they were using crystal power to heal one another. They stayed far away from those in the valley. Many in this group became the witches, healers, and shamans of later lifetimes.

Our lives during Atlantis were of two women cave-dwellers who had reached the highest regard as healers. They lived during the era of the *Trine Crystal*, named for the huge three-sided pyramid crystal discovered in one of the largest caverns. The Trine Crystal was left by the visitor beings and its powers were so great that neither the cave-dwellers, nor those in the valley, could fully understand its powers and how to direct them. We were sisters, and as one-unit, we healed those from the caves who needed us. During that lifetime, the Trine Crystal began generating an abundance of power and the lands began to shake, causing enormous tidals of the waters that surrounded the island itself. The entire continent was destroyed, sinking into the oceans. Our lives were filled with love for each other. Our lives were cut short in the destruction of the Atlantis Island.

What were our names?

Your name was Athena and ours was Meratta.

Author's Note

I continued receiving insights and various details of my lifetimes from David. After his final channeling of lifetimes, I researched dates, locations, names and facts. I was able to find many of the needed records and data to substantiate much of this channeled information. I asked one last question of David in the beginning of February 2013: Are there any other lifetimes which I should know about in order for me to complete my, our, book?

You have had many lifetimes, Barbara, some with us and many without. We know you want to learn of lifetimes in which we have learned our matas together, and to feel complete with your life as Barbara. We have chosen matas of completion, a desire to live together in a loving relationship until our souls pass into the Oneness together. It has taken many lifetimes to accomplish a lifetime in which we lived to have children together and live into our older years. Our lifetime as Barbara and David met that desire. The thread that lies between us and your soul is a strong one. We have experienced many lifetimes together, both on Earth and in other realms. We see more lifetimes for us together as well.

As you continue to meditate, ask for guidance from within to guide you to other lifetimes to be included in your book. You will find the visions and research you need to confirm your lifetimes and write your book. I will always be near you....

Toward the end of my channeling, I received this communication:

We will always be with you, Barbara... always near you, just ask. Your book will be a great comfort to many. You can use your lifetimes to share with others and show how our free choices direct our growth. It will be read by many who will use the information for their own guidance. Weave a tale of love, Barbara... for your lifetimes have been evolving in grace and love. You are a Light, a Soul Light... from the Oneness.

I began piecing together my writing to form *The Pact: Messages from the Other Side*. As I received more information through dreams, meditations, and visions throughout my writing, I weaved it together with my current lifetime with David. As I did this, I realized: *The insights, wisdom, and love between our souls originates from the struggles we experience in each lifetime in order to learn our soul lessons.* I learned why it was necessary for my son, Rich, and my dear husband, David, to leave my current reality when they did. I have gained an enormous amount of respect and love for all of life by being open to channeling spirit, and I will always feel David's presence near.

David Lee Sinor

Lifetime Identification Chart

Presented	Name	Identification	Records
Atlantis (A Million Years Ago)	Athena	Barbara	
	Meratta	David	
	Amma	Cindy (?)	
The Americas 1675-1700s AD	Anna Jo Brackston	Barbara	Yes
	John Brackston	?	Yes
	June Anne Livingston	David's mother	?
	James Livingston	David	?
Lakota Tribe 1731-1790s AD	Hawk Spirit	Barbara	
	Rides with Wind	Richard	
	Little Foot	David	
	Chief Elk Foot	?	
	Chief Black Feather	?	
Asia Minor 300 BC	Mia	Barbara	
	Kya	Richard	
	Celtic Warrior	?	
Mongolia 1192-1232 AD	Tolui	Barbara	Yes
	Sorghaghtani	David	Yes
	Temujin	?	Yes
San Francisco 1871-1906 AD	Carrie Anna Williamson	Barbara	Yes
	William Paxton Muir	David	Yes
	John Williamson, M.D.	Nancy	Yes
	June Evington Williamson	Cindy	Yes
	Clara W. Muir	?	Yes
	Walter A. Muir	?	Yes
Egypt 18th Dynasty 1500 BC	Iset (Isis)	Barbara	Yes
	Gombat	David	
	Thutmose II	Richard	Yes
	Nuni	?	
	Chief Kabin	?	
	Thutmose III	?	Yes
	Hatshepsut	?	Yes

*Documentation from Birth, Death, Event records and Encyclopedia entries

References

Aldred, C. (1951). *New kingdom art in ancient Egypt during the eighteenth dynasty: 1590 to 1315 B.C.* London: A. Tiranti.

Dass, R. (2010, March 1). *Dying is absolutely safe.* Retrieved from http://www.ramdass.org/dying-is-absolutely-safe/

Groban, J. (2010). *Illuminations.* Burbank, CA: 143 Records.

Lazaris, & Pursel, J. (1988). *Lazaris interviews: Book II.* Beverly Hills, CA: Concept Synergy Pub.

Mountain, D. O. (1999). *The invitation.* San Francisco: HarperONE.

Sams, J., & Carson, D. (1988). *Medicine cards: The discovery of power through the ways of animals.* Sante Fe, N.M: Bear & Co.

Slater, Paula B.: www.PaulaSlater.com

Starhawk. (1979). *The spiral dance.* New York: Harper & Row.

Stewart, R., Slade, R., Golder, T., Goswami, A. (2009). *The quantum activist.* United States: Intention Media.

Acknowledgements

Oriah, *The Invitation* © 1999. Published by HarperONE, San Francisco. All rights reserved. Presented with permission of the author. www.oriah.org

Illustrations

Barbara Hutchins Sinor iii

Illustration of Plato's Atlantis 6

1961 - Barbara, Paula, and David 25

Our 1959 Chevy El Camino 27

Cabin in the early 1700s 42

Bighorn Medicine Wheel (Wyoming) 46

Lakota Oglala girl (John C.H. Grabill, 1891) 49

A band of Celtic warriors 58

Cessna 175 (1960) 62

Mongolian Yurt 66

Mongolian Warriors 68

Cable car in San Francisco (1901) 75

Cliff House (1902) 77

Victorian Era Women 82

Our 1991 Wedding; Paula, Barbara, and Nancy 84

Our 1994 Hawaii Vacation 84

Burning of San Francisco after 1906 Earthquake (Arnold Genthe) 93

The God Amun-Ra 97

Nubia circa 1500 BC 98

King Thutmose II 101

David and Barbara in Redwoods................................. 104

The Goddess Isis.. 108

Queen Hatshepsut... 109

Pyramids in Nubia... 113

Queen Isis.. 114

King Thutmose III 117

David Lee Sinor.. 171

Photograph credits for Chapters Eleven and Twelve are attributed to the book *New Kingdom Art in Ancient Egypt During the Eighteenth Dynasty*, Cyril Aldred, 1951, Alec Tiranti Ltd., London. Reproduced with permission.

In order presented:

Plate #35; The God Amen-Ra as depicted during the reign of Thutmose III, statue found in Karnak in 1926. Photo, Metropolitan Museum of Art, NY.

Plate #12; Alabaster statue of Thutmose II excavated at Karnak in 1905. Photo, Cairo Museum.

Plate #154; The Goddess Isis as worshiped by Egyptians during the 18th Dynasty. Statue is from the innermost treasury. Photo, Griffith Institute, Oxford.

Plate #21; Queen Hatshepsut during her rule as pharaoh during the reign of Thutmose III, statue in white marble excavated in 1845. One of the few pieces of art following the order from Thutmose III to destroy her likeness from all depictions as pharaoh. Photo, Metropolitan Museum of Art, NY.

Plate #34; Queen Isis in a black granite statue, made by order of Thutmose III after his mother's death, excavated in 1904. Photo, Cairo Museum.

Plate #39; King Thutmose III in black granite. Photo, Museo Egizio, Turin.

About the Author

Barbara Sinor, Ph.D. is a retired psychotherapist living in northern California. Sinor's many books are highly endorsed in the inspirational, adult children of alcoholics, childhood abuse/incest, and addiction recovery genres.

Dr. Sinor encourages your comments and can be contacted through her website at www.DrSinor.com. Her work also appears in the quarterly *Recovering the Self: A Journal of Hope and Healing*, as well as other magazines, newsletters, and blogs. Contact Barbara through her website regarding workshops surrounding this book's content and how to connect with departed loved ones and/or realize past lifetimes.

Dr. Sinor is currently writing her first fiction novel titled, *Finding Destiny*. Here is a brief description from the book's cover:

> When life throws us a curve, is it best to dive into a corner to retreat until the frayed ends of an unknown world are magically mended? We have all tried this ruse; it usually does not unwind the dramas that so cleverly worked their way into our lives. No, retreat is not a decision for brave women who meet each day armed with an inner mantra to squeeze every drop of existence and *joie de vivre!* from their being. Destiny was one of those young women who accepted Fate's responsibility, properly carrying it upon her shoulders to climb over each obstruction placed in her path. She had learned to stare Fear in the eye, defying his stubborn stance to reach from deep within for enough self-love to snide his confrontation. Yes, Destiny was a rare young woman, indeed.

CPSIA information can be obtained at www.ICGtesting.com
Printed in the USA
BVOW11s0213110414

350253BV00002B/3/P

9 781615 992140